D1592179

HEBREW
MANUSCRIPTS

The Power of Script and Image

HEBREW MANUSCRIPTS

The Power of Script and Image

Ilana Tahan

The British Library

First published 2007 by
The British Library
96 Euston Road
London NW1 2DB

British Library Cataloguing-in-Publication Data
A Catalogue record for this book is available
from The British Library

ISBN 978 0 7123 4921 5

Designed and typeset by Bobby & Co, London
Printed and bound in Italy by Trento S.r.l.

OPPOSITE
Ark of the Covenant flanked by cherubim
North French Hebrew Miscellany
France
c. 1278–98
165 x 125 mm
MS Add. 11639, f. 522r (detail)

HALF-TITLE PAGE
Frontispiece to the Book of Deuteronomy
The Duke of Sussex German Pentateuch
Germany
c. 1300
230 x 165 mm
MS Add. 15282, f. 238r (detail)

TITLE PAGE
Beginning of Ecclesiastes
The Duke of Sussex German Pentateuch
Germany
c. 1300
230 x 165 mm
MS Add. 15282, f. 302r (detail)

FRONT JACKET
Jerusalem and the Temple
The Leipnik Hagadah
Altona
1740
MS Sloane 3173, f. 34r

BACK JACKET
Noah's Ark
North French Hebrew Miscellany
France
c. 1278–98
165 x 125 mm
MS Add. 11639, f. 521r (detail)

Contents

אחי יוסף · ויגער בו אביו · וימצאהו איש · אחי רועים הוא

Introduction

With the exception of the Dead Sea Scrolls, which are to date the earliest extant Hebrew texts copied by hand (c. 2nd century BC to the 1st century AD), Hebrew manuscripts are largely vestiges of the Jewish diaspora communities that sprang up around the Mediterranean basin in the centuries following the destruction of the Second Temple in AD 70. With Judea devastated and Jerusalem, the heart of Jewish religious and spiritual life, in ruins, it was the book that was to assume the pivotal role in disseminating and propagating the religion, traditions and values of the dispersed Jewish people. It was after the Jewish world adopted the codex in the 8th century AD that handwritten books came to be seen as the most efficient channels for transmitting the Jewish sacred texts and the laws that regulated daily life, and as useful vehicles for expressing the cultural and social aspirations of Jews everywhere. Above all, books ensured that Hebrew, the holy language of Judaism, continued to live on, despite the vagaries and uncertainties of Jewish life. Astonishingly, for almost two millennia, Jewish communities in all corners of the world continued to pray, compose and copy texts in a language that had no defined geographical borders, nor a state to safeguard and perpetuate it. This in itself must be one of the most extraordinary and unique phenomena in the history of the written word.

Books became priceless and cherished possessions that accompanied their Jewish owners wherever they went, be it on voluntary wanderings and peregrinations, or forced exile into the unknown. Hebrew manuscripts are thus closely linked to the destiny of the Jewish people, providing palpable testimonies of their infinitely complex and trying history.

An estimated 80,000 Hebrew manuscript volumes have survived, of which approximately 40,000 are medieval. These are preserved in over six hundred public and private collections and libraries worldwide. Some scholars argue that this figure represents merely a fraction of the real number of Hebrew manuscripts that were produced over the course of the centuries. Apart from a negligible quantity of existing papyri and scroll fragments, there is no tangible evidence of any Hebrew book production for the eight hundred-year period from the mid-2nd century to the end of the 9th century AD. This fact has preoccupied scholars for many decades, and is still awaiting satisfactory explanation. Thus, the bulk of extant Hebrew manuscripts represents, in effect, the output of the last six centuries of the medieval era alone.

Although historical factors, such as expulsions, persecutions, pogroms, censorship, confiscations and public burnings, have all played a part in the unfortunate loss of innumerable Hebrew hand-copied books, many volumes have simply perished through extensive wear and tear. Whereas Christian and, to some extent, Islamic manuscripts were made chiefly for royalty and learned, wealthy patrons, and were duly preserved in royal and private libraries, monasteries or mosques, Hebrew manuscripts were often copied by ordinary people for their private use, a fact generally attributed to the widespread literacy among Jews and their classless social order.

Constant handling of manuscripts inevitably resulted in their rapid deterioration and damage, but the Jewish emphasis on the written word means that considerable quantities of worn-out and damaged Hebrew manuscripts have nevertheless survived. In addition, Hebrew is regarded as the language of God and the Hebrew alphabet as holy, so sacred texts written in Hebrew, and documents that might contain God's name or divine invocations, cannot be disposed of, even after they have served their purpose. Indeed, to the 80,000 volumes noted earlier must be added a substantial number of manuscript fragments that have been found in various *genizot* (literally hiding-places). A *genizah* (singular) is essentially a depository for damaged Hebrew books that are no longer in use. According to Jewish tradition, such writings must be kept in a storeroom, usually in a synagogue, prior to being given a proper cemetery burial.

Undoubtedly the largest and most comprehensive archive of discarded Hebrew manuscripts is the Cairo *genizah*, which was discovered during the 19th century in the Ben Ezra Synagogue in Fustat, Old Cairo, and partly in the Jewish cemetery located there. This vast accumulation of religious and secular documents comprises some 210,000 fragments dating from around AD 870 to 1880.

OPPOSITE
Scenes from Genesis
The Golden Hagadah
Catalonia, Spain
c. 1320
247 x 198 mm
MS Add. 27210, f. 10v

Apart from providing a mine of information on the social and economic life in the Mediterranean world during the medieval era, this archive also throws light on the reading habits of Jews who lived there at the time.

Hebrew hand-copied books that were produced during the Middle Ages encompass a wide range of religious and secular texts. As the Hebrew Bible is central to Judaism and has consistently served as a prime source for learning and study, the copying of Bibles, both in their entirety and in their constituent parts, continued throughout the medieval era. Known to the Jews as *Tanakh*, the Hebrew Bible comprises twenty-four books arranged into three major sections: *Torah*, or the Law, deemed the most sacred; *Nevi'im*, the Prophets; and *Ketuvim*, meaning Writings. Every so often biblical codices had masoretic notation or rabbinic commentaries added in the margins. Especially popular was the commentary by Rabbi Solomon ben Itzhaki of Troyes, known as Rashi (1040–1105), probably the greatest medieval interpreter of the Hebrew Scriptures. Approximately a quarter of all Hebrew manuscripts now extant are Bibles and biblical commentaries. Other religious texts that were often copied by hand include rabbinic and legal works, liturgies and liturgical poetry, and Kabbalistic and mystical writings. The secular gamut embraces philosophical, scientific and medical texts, dictionaries, grammars and lexicons, diaries, communal ledgers and personal letters.

As Jews treasured their manuscripts, they often had them beautified with decorations and pictures. Increasing their visual appeal would also have enhanced their value, especially if they were made of parchment and were written by professional scribes. A manuscript penned by a single copyist was considered particularly valuable. In the medieval period, the writings most frequently decorated and illuminated were biblical codices and liturgies, legal codes, philosophical treatises, and medical and scientific works. Occasionally, such works would be illustrated, but in general, illustrations of rituals and biblical narratives were most common in Passover Hagadot (service books). With few exceptions, Bibles were rarely illustrated. Commissioned and owned by affluent patrons, medieval Hebrew illuminated manuscripts were considered important status symbols and art objects in their own right. Proudly displayed and carefully looked after, these splendid books were parted with only in times of hardship.

The inclusion of imagery in Hebrew manuscripts begs two fundamental questions. First, can figurative painting be reconciled with the injunction in the second biblical commandment, which explicitly forbids it?

> Thou shalt not make unto thee a graven image nor any likeness of anything that is in heaven above, or that is in the earth beneath, or that is in the water under the earth; thou shalt not bow down thyself unto them, nor serve them. (Exodus 20: 4–5)

In Judaism, for example, a strict ban on any decoration still applies to the copying of a Torah scroll.

The answer to the first question lies in the biblical passage itself: imagery is not permissible if used in idol worshipping. Accordingly, not all forms of artistic expression are forbidden in Jewish law. In general, rabbinic authorities permitted, albeit reluctantly, two-dimensional figurative representations, but three-dimensional objects, such as sculptures, were strictly prohibited.

As to the second question – is Judaism congenial to art? – it has been a long-held view that Jews considered art, especially figurative art, objectionable, but this seems to be erroneous. Indeed, as far back as biblical times it appears that artistic endeavour was, in fact, much appreciated. The biblical text in which God instructs Moses how to adorn and decorate the holy Tabernacle and its furnishings, is definitely a case in point (Exodus chapter 25).

Over time, but especially in the medieval period, rabbis and sages who may have been initially averse to artistic forms began to see art as a means of enriching spirituality rather than an impediment to it. They interpreted the verse 'This is my God and I will praise Him; my father's God and I will exalt Him' (Exodus 15: 2) as an exhortation to glorify the Lord through visual splendour. Thus, the concept of *hidur mitsvah* (beautification of the commandment) became the underlying justification for adorning and embellishing ceremonial artefacts, manuscripts of sacred and religious texts, and other objects employed in the Jewish ritual. Worshipping and venerating the Creator through visual beauty would bring one closer to His divine mercy and His commandments. In his *Sefer Ma'aseh Efod (The Story of Efodi)* the Spanish Jewish philosopher Profiat Duran (d. 1414) explains how art can inspire and stimulate holiness and learning:

BELOW
Adam and Eve
Code of Law of Jacob ben Asher
Italy
1475
350 x 265 mm
MS Harley 5717 (v. 2), f. 5v (detail)

> Study should always be in beautiful books, pleasant for their beauty and the splendour of their scripts and parchments, with elegant ornament and covers. And the places for study should be desirable, the study halls beautifully built so that people's love and desire for study will increase... It is also obligatory and appropriate to enhance the books of God and to direct oneself to their beauty, splendour and loveliness. Just as God wished to adorn the place of His Sanctuary with gold, silver and precious stones, so is this appropriate for His holy books, especially for the book that is 'His Sanctuary'.

The earliest decorated Hebrew manuscripts were produced between the 9th and 12th centuries AD in the Islamic Near East, mainly in Egypt and Palestine. These were largely biblical codices, which shared many artistic and stylistic features with contemporary Qur'ans. Owing to these marked ornamental similarities, it has been suggested that these Bibles may have been written for the Karaites, a Jewish schismatic sect founded in the 8th century AD, who nurtured a close kinship to Muslim culture. The striking Karaite Exodus with Islamic-style carpet pages and Hebrew text transcribed in Arabic characters (*figs.* 1–4) highlights this affinity.

Islam's aniconic approach had a profound and lasting impact on Hebrew manuscripts created in Muslim lands. Like Qur'ans, early Hebrew Bibles are entirely devoid of human and animal imagery, and their ornamentation is overtly functional. Elements emphasized in Qur'anic art are adapted to the Jewish manuscript context, as illustrated, for instance, in the First and Second Gaster Bibles (*figs.* 5–7).

During the 14th century an important school of Hebrew manuscript painting developed in Yemen, reaching its pinnacle in the second half of the 15th century. Surviving manuscripts from the latter period, such as the famous Sana'a Pentateuch (*figs.* 9–14) present a skilful blend of Jewish artistic elements and adapted Islamic motifs. Although here too human depictions are banned and the decoration is rooted in functionality, the incorporation of micrographic fish patterns (created out of minute lettering) represents a departure from the stern anti-figurative attitude.

Not all Hebrew manuscripts created in Islamic countries lack representational art. A rarity is the text illustration showing the holy vessels in an 11th-century codex from Persia (*fig.* 8). Other noteworthy exceptions are the striking prototypes with copious figurative imagery that were produced in Iran during the 17th century. These are predominantly copies of biblical epics by famous Persian Jewish poets, penned in Judaeo-Persian and elaborately illustrated in a manner influenced by the Persian court art of Isfahan, which flourished during the Safavid dynasty (1501–1722). *The Book of Conquest* (*figs.* 125–126) provides a splendid example of this unique style of Hebrew miniature painting.

In Western Christendom the illumination of Hebrew books began around the 13th century, continuing until the close of the 15th century. Throughout this period schools of Hebrew manuscript painting were established in Ashkenaz, specifically France and Germany, in Sephard (Spain and Portugal) and in Italy.

The Sephardi manuscript legacy mirrors the cross-cultural ties between Jews, Christians and Muslims during the ongoing Christian reconquest of the Iberian territories from the Moorish states of north Africa. In Spain the production of Hebrew painted codices lasted nearly 160 years, but the fierce anti-Jewish riots of 1391 brought it finally to a close. A century later Spanish Jewry was eventually expelled from the land. A thriving school of Hebrew illumination operated at Lisbon in Portugal from about 1469, but its success was short-lived, for in 1497 the Portuguese Jews were forced either to convert or leave for good.

Peculiar to the decoration of Spanish Hebrew Bibles is the absence of narrative elements and human imagery, and an apparent predilection for Islamic artistic forms. This is surprising as most of the existing ornamented codices emanate from areas within Spain where Muslim dominance had ended long before. Admittedly, in 1232, when the earliest Hebrew decorated Bible was completed in Castile, Christian hegemony in the region was almost two hundred years old. An example illustrating this unusual preference for Islamic as opposed to Gothic motifs is the First Ibn Merwas Bible, signed in Toledo in 1300 (*fig.* 115). All the more intriguing is the anti-figurative approach and the presence of Islamic features in Hebrew Bibles from 14th-century Catalonia, a region with very strong Christian traditions, where Islamic culture played barely any role at all. Some scholars maintain that the Islamic component in Spanish Bibles is an obvious expression of the prolonged Jewish-Arab cultural symbiosis in Muslim Spain, and of the eagerness among the Sephardi elite to keep alive the Judaeo-Islamic heritage. This symbiotic coexistence, known as the Golden Age of Spanish Jewry, lasted over four hundred years (*c.* 8th to 12th century). The unique Temple iconography imbued with messianic significance, which prefaces Catalonian Bibles (*figs* 36–42), was apparently influenced by the Sanctuary descriptions in works by Moses Maimonides (1135–1204), whose rationalistic outlook was grounded in the Judaeo-Islamic coexistence.

The opulence and refinement of Hebrew painted codices from Portugal are unrivalled. Their dazzling displays of floral and faunal motifs, laced with intricate filigree penwork and burnished gold script, more than make up for the complete absence of narrative illustrations. The lavishness of their illuminated pages attests to the highest level of craftsmanship from a team of consummate artisans. The iconic Lisbon Bible (*figs* 43–50), the sumptuous Lisbon Maimonides (*figs* 99–102), and the fine Almanzi and Sussex Pentateuchs (*figs* 51–52 and 53–54 respectively) were created in a 15th-century Lisbon workshop, whose output is a genuine reflection of the privileged and sophisticated community it served.

Hebrew painted manuscripts originating in France, Germany and Italy show great similarities in decoration to contemporary Christian manuscripts from the same region. Their style and methods of production were profoundly affected by the artistic currents in the host cultures. Thus manuscripts from Ashkenaz tend to follow the Gothic styles fashionable in France and Germany during the 13th and 14th centuries. Remarkable specimens include the Sussex German Pentateuch, with illuminations executed in a pronounced south German style (*figs.* 30–32), and the exquisitely wrought North French Miscellany (*figs* 106–110), with numerous stunning biblical illustrations. Some elegantly illuminated specimens from Italy bear the artistic imprints of the Renaissance (*figs* 70–72, 103) and the humanist movements (*figs* 67–68) that flourished there in the 15th century; others mirror regional styles, such as that of Ferrara (*figs* 59–60).

Although a Jewish scribe had the crucial role of overseeing the execution of the entire manuscript, unless he was also an artist, he would normally have entrusted the decorations to professional illuminators. In some medieval Hebrew manuscripts the illuminations were in fact executed by non-Jewish artisans, which clearly testifies to cross-cultural ties between Jewish scribes and Christian illuminators. Notable examples include the manuscripts of the *Guide to the Perplexed* (*figs* 113–114), the legal code of Isaiah of Trani (*figs* 97–98), and the Ashkenazi Hagadah (*figs* 93–96), to name just a few.

In Hebrew manuscript ornamentation the script itself is undoubtedly the most significant component. At every step Jewish scribes emphasize the power of words through the letters of the Hebrew alphabet. One cannot but marvel at the perfect evenness of Sephardi letters (*figs* 44, 88) and the beautifully tapered Ashkenazi characters (*figs* 57, 108). Jewish copyists strove to enhance the beauty of the Hebrew script through a diversity of techniques: exaggerated letter serifs (*fig.* 83), display lettering (*figs* 76, 96), ligatures (*fig.* 89), and scripts of different sizes lying side by side (*fig.* 111) fulfil an aesthetic role, underscoring the importance of text through visual channels.

Visual impact also comes from the decorations that invariably grace the incipits (opening pages) of many a Hebrew manuscript. Since the Hebrew alphabet lacks upper-case characters, Jewish scribes customarily decorated the first words of text rather than individual letters. Particularly fine examples can be found in Italian Hebrew Bibles (*figs* 19–20, 27–28, 59–60), and also in liturgical manuscripts (*figs* 66, 70, 75). Only seldom, in an attempt to emulate practices employed by their Christian counterparts, did Jewish scribes embellish first letters (*figs* 21–22, 95).

Nowhere is Hebrew script more aesthetically engaging than in micrography. Unique to Jewish art, micrography is the weaving of minuscule lettering into abstract, geometric and figurative designs. This scribal practice, which continues to this day, started around the 9th century in Egypt and Palestine, then gradually spread to Europe and Yemen, reaching its pinnacle between the 13th and 15th centuries. Initially, Jewish scribes employed text from the *Masorah* (body of rules on the reading, writing and intonation of the biblical text) to devise micrographic patterns, but over time they began relying on other sources, a particular favourite being the Book of Psalms (*figs.* 9–10). Codices from Castelon d'Ampurias in Spain (*figs.* 116 and 118) contain striking micrographic patterning, but even more impressive are the complex and elaborate designs in manuscripts created in Ashkenaz, particularly Germany (*figs.* 119–122).

It is in the Hagadah that the art of the illuminator attains new heights. Perhaps because it was intended mainly for use at home and its purpose was educational, Jewish scribes and artists felt completely free to illustrate the Passover Hagadah. A mosaic of biblical passages, legends, blessings and rituals, its text has been a fertile source of inspiration, offering wide scope for creativity. Most Sephardi Hagadot from 14th-century Catalonia feature text and ritual illustrations, and are either prefaced with or appended by cycles of full-page miniatures based on episodes from Exodus and sometimes Genesis. This pictorial arrangement is best illustrated in the famed Golden Hagadah (*fig.* 81).

Some scholars believe that the preliminary cycles were inspired by similar images in Latin psalters; others, however, contend that the biblical imagery found in psalters has theological implications, whereas the illustrations in Hagadot lack all doctrinal significance. An interesting theory concerning the origins of the biblical cycles is that they are rooted in Gothic art and were strongly influenced by rabbinic interpretations. The Barcelona Hagadah (*figs.* 90–92) lacks the characteristic full-page biblical cycles, being instead endowed with a panoramic sequence of ritual and text illustrations set either within ornamented panels or amidst marginal foliage and decorative grotesques. The visual power of its illustrations is unique among Sephardi Hagadot.

After the invention of printing Jews kept alive the tradition of manuscript production and the art of illumination in the centuries that followed, producing various texts, including those required for religious practice, and also illuminated marriage contracts (particularly popular in Italy during the 17th and 18th centuries), and decorated Esther scrolls (the biblical book of Esther, greatly in demand from the 16th century onwards). The beautiful Marelli Scroll is one of four surviving Esther scrolls from the 16th century (*figs.* 137–138).

The revival of Hebrew manuscript art in the 18th century, which some scholars regard as a unique phenomenon in Jewish art, began in Austria, Bohemia and Moravia, gradually spreading to Germany and the Netherlands. This revival, which some have called the 'Jewish Renaissance', has been linked to the emergence of a wealthy class of central European 'court Jews' who served their Gentile rulers and concurrently acted as representatives of their own communities. Influenced by the fashion prevailing in their Christian environment, they began to commission painted manuscripts for everyday and special occasions, Hagadot, prayer books and other texts, leading apparently to the formation of a school of professional scribe-artists. The imagery in these manuscripts was drawn from printed books, particularly the 1695 and 1712 Amsterdam Hagadot, which the copyist-illuminators presented in a fresh, individualistic style. One of the most beautiful examples from the so-called Jewish Renaissance period is the Leipnik Hagadah (*figs.* 127–128).

During the Middle Ages the art of the book became the centre of all artistic creativity for Jewish communities in the Near East and Europe. Adorning and decorating their Bibles, liturgies and legal codes became one of the most meaningful ways in which to express their belief in the Creator and the written word. Living in a medieval non-Jewish environment, Jewish scribes and artists were often influenced by the contemporary artistic trends of the countries in which they lived. Consequently, two important traditions of Hebrew illuminated manuscripts can be distinguished – one showing the influence of the Muslim artistic style prevailing in the Near East, and the other revealing a close affinity with the styles of illumination in Christian Europe.

The British Library's uniquely versatile collection of Hebrew manuscripts contains striking and beautifully crafted examples from all the schools of Hebrew illumination that flourished in Europe and the Near East during the Middle Ages. Post-medieval 17th-, 18th- and 19th-century Hebrew illumination from the European continent and other parts of the world is also well represented. The 145 colour images selected for inclusion in this volume are vivid evidence of Jewish artistic creativity over the centuries, and afford a close view into the rich vein of rituals and traditions.

הא לחמא עניא

THE MANUSCRIPTS

OPPOSITE
Family *Seder*
Barcelona Hagadah
Barcelona, Spain
1370
MS Add. 14761, f. 28v

ABOVE
Unleavened bread
Hispano-Moresque Hagadah
Castile, Spain
c. 1300
160 x 120 mm
MS Or 2737, f. 22r (detail)

1–2 Carpet pages
Karaite Book of Exodus
Palestine or Egypt
c. 10th century
235 x 175 mm
MS Or. 2540, ff. 2v-3r

Regarded as one of the earliest illuminated Bibles in the Hebrew collection of the British Library, this important Karaite manuscript has carpet pages decorated with stylized flowers, drawn in black ink, and geometric borders in gold executed in Islamic style. The marginal palmette on the left-hand page is a motif inspired by Qur'anic art. This was one of 145 mostly Karaite manuscripts that the British Museum acquired in July 1882, from the late Moses W. Shapira, a well-known antiquarian book-dealer from Jerusalem. Shapira had managed to obtain this collection partly at Hit in Iraq and partly at Cairo in Egypt. A Jewish sect founded by Anan ben David in Babylonia

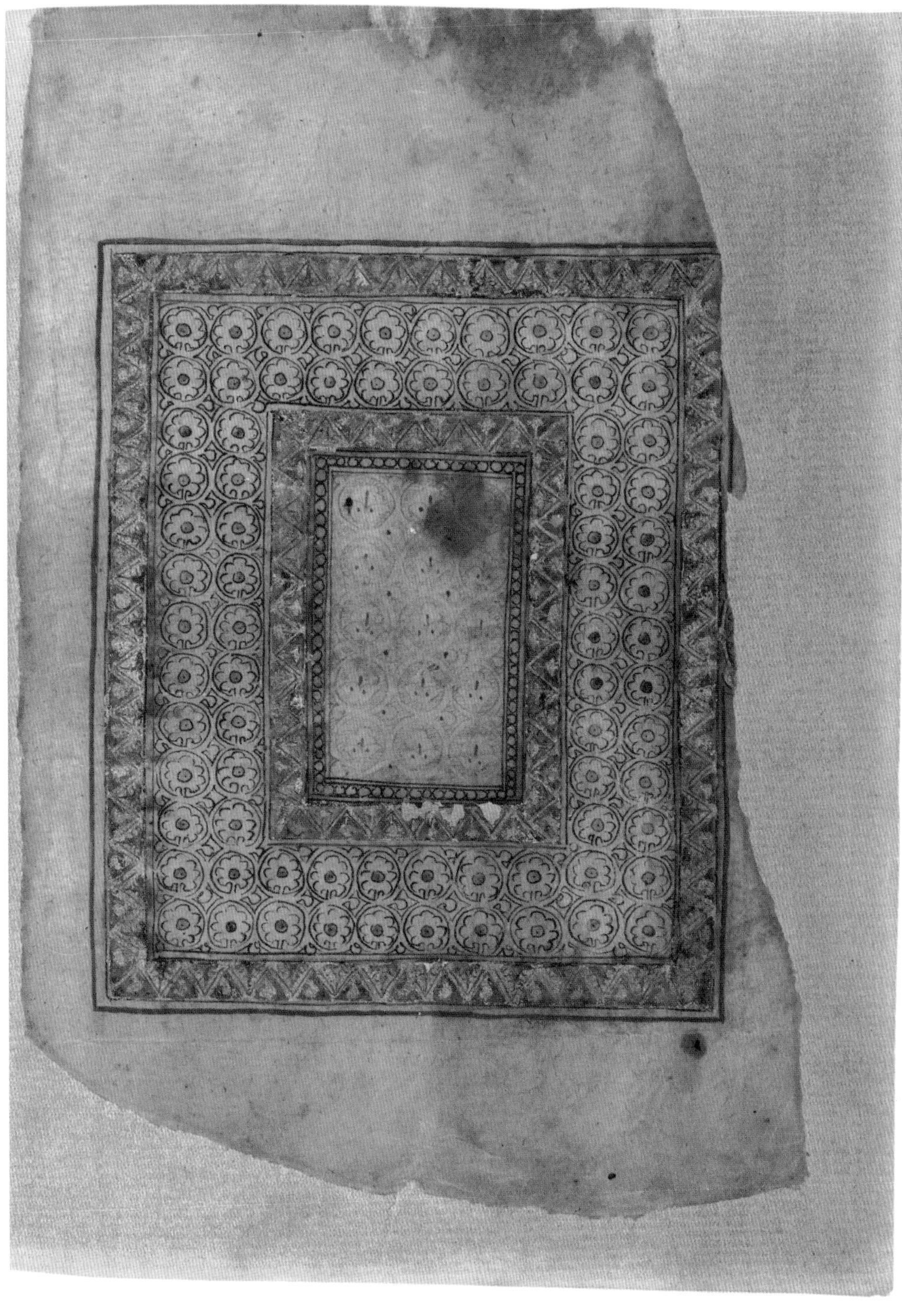

in the 8th century AD, the Karaites broke away from mainstream Judaism, accepting the Hebrew Bible (*Tanakh*) as their only norm of religious authority while rejecting rabbinic tradition. This led to a concentration on the study of the scriptural text, on its 'correct' translation, pronunciation and interpretation. The Karaite movement waned following the destruction of their centres of scholarship in Palestine by the Crusaders in 1099. Over time, its main centre moved to Turkey, then in the 18th century to Lithuania and Crimea, and now it is in Israel.

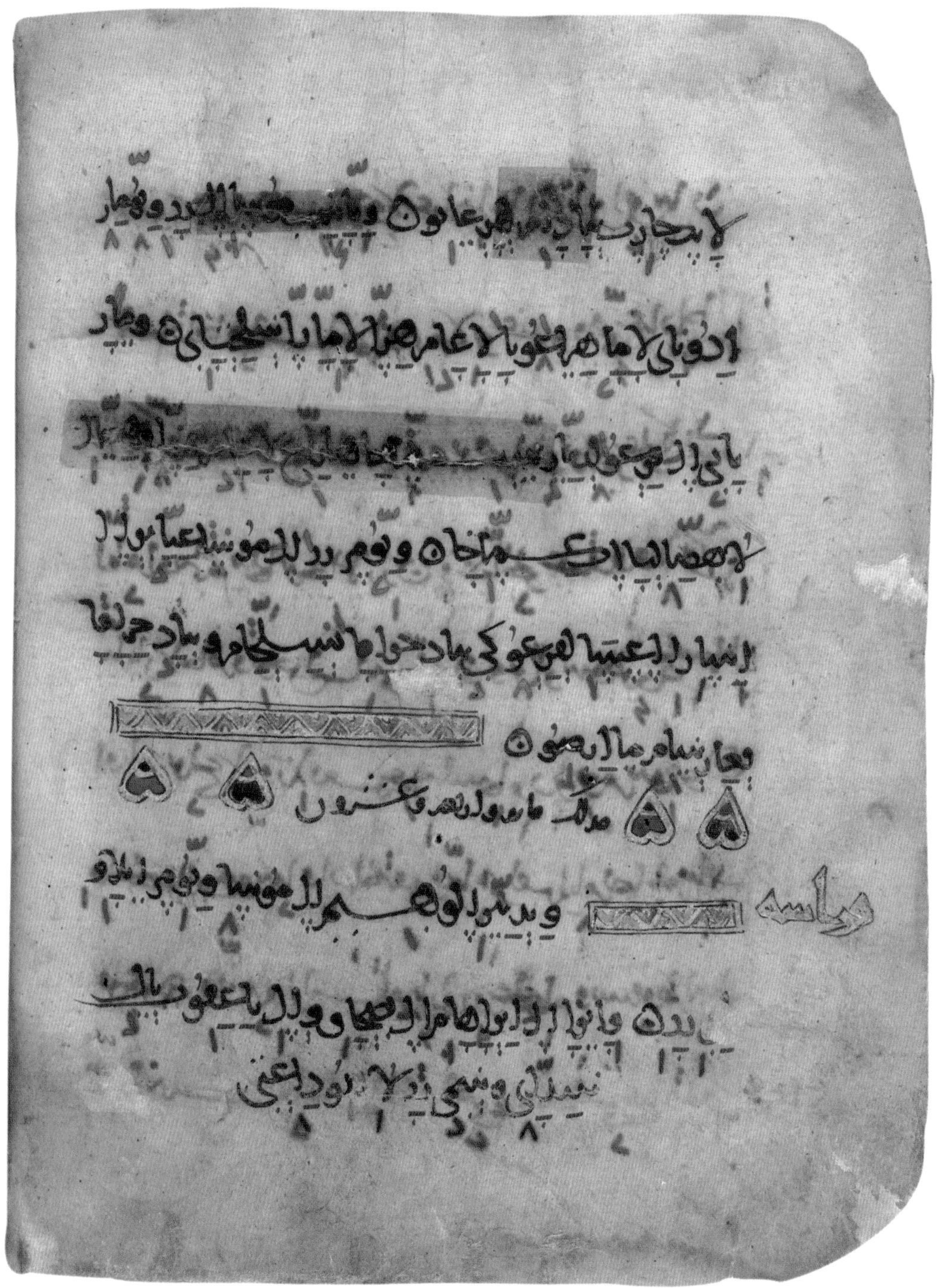

3 Pericope *Va-Era*
Karaite Book of Exodus
Palestine or Egypt
c. 10th century
235 x 175 mm
MS Or. 2540, f. 15v

The Hebrew biblical text on this page was copied in Arabic *Naskhi* script. The vowels (according to the Tiberian system) were added in red ink, while the accents and diacritical marks were penned in green. As in early Qur'ans, the ornamentation in this manuscript is primarily functional, filling out incomplete lines or indicating major textual divisions. Typical space fillers, adapted from Muslim designs, include stylized foliage, floral and abstract patterns, zig-zag bands and geometric interlacing enhanced in gold. The marginal gilded Hebrew word *parashah* (portion) penned in Arabic script marks the beginning of pericope *Va-Era* (Exodus 6:2).

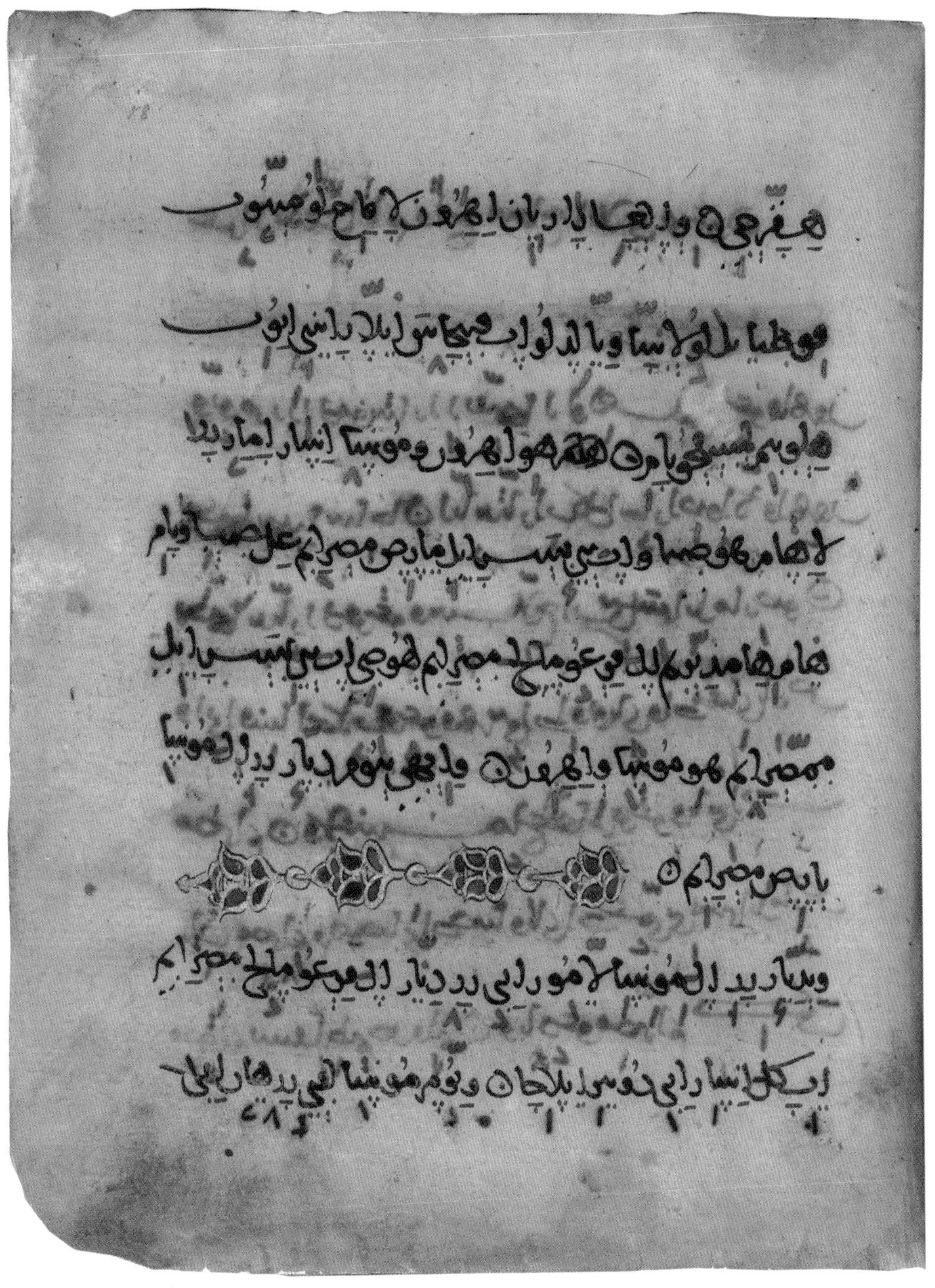

The Hebrew biblical text in this manuscript was penned in Arabic script. The Karaites often transcribed the Hebrew Bible into Arabic, perhaps as an attempt to arrive at a correct reading tradition for the Scriptures, which they considered superior to the masoretic text devised by the Rabbanites. The dainty gold-tinted palmette chain seen in the lower half of the page is a space filler marking the end of Exodus 6:28.

4 Beginning of Exodus
Karaite Book of Exodus
Palestine or Egypt
c. 10th century
235 x 175 mm
MS Or. 2540, f. 18r

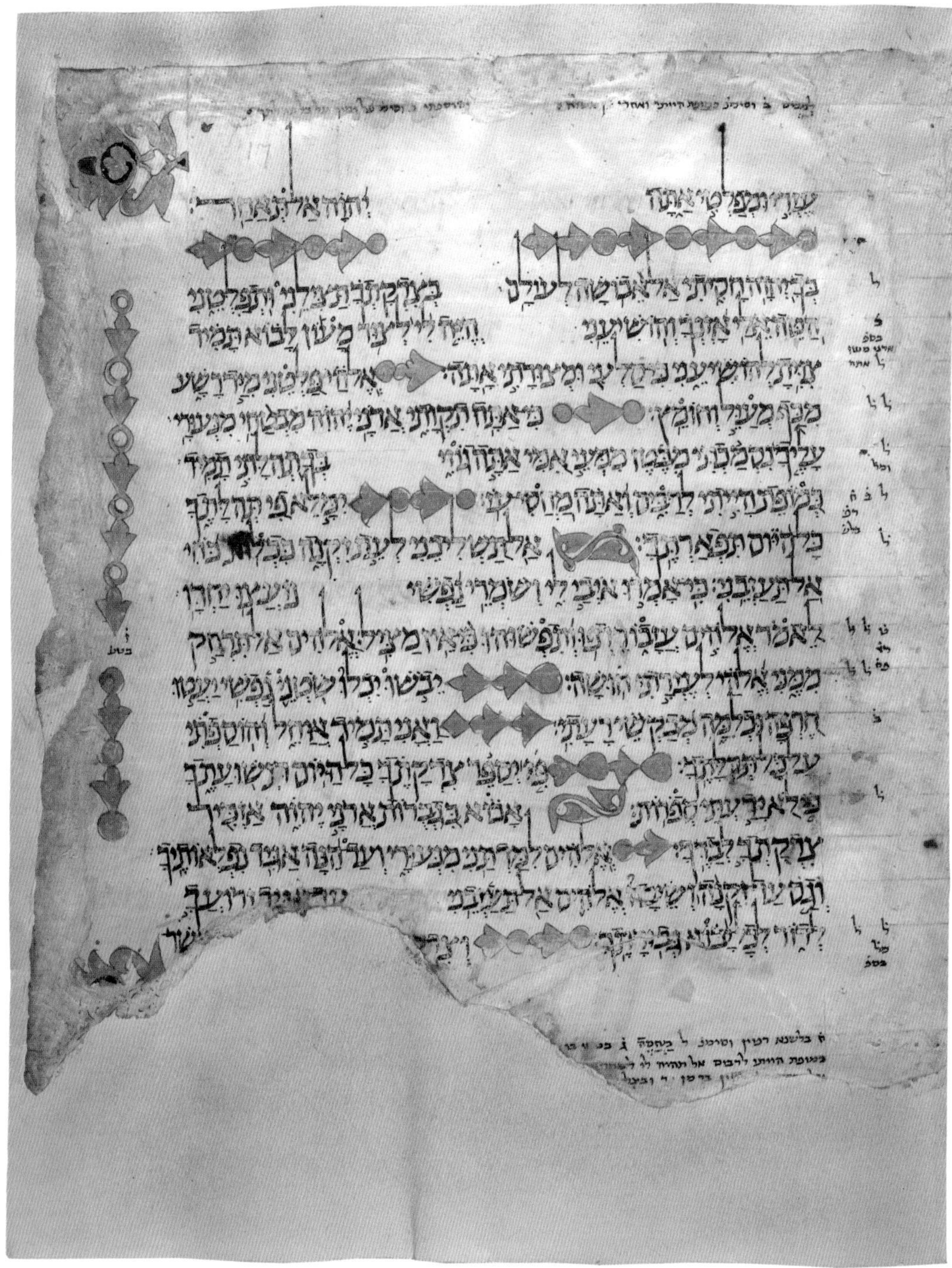

5 Psalm 71 with ornamental fillers
First Gaster Bible
Hagiographa
Egypt?
9th or 10th century
330 x 242 mm
MS Or. 9879, f. 17r

In this codex the Psalms are laid out in hemistich form, each line being divided in two unequal halves. Textual gaps and margins are decorated with gilded motifs in Islamic style. These include undulating scrolls and spirals, foliage, interwoven buds and palmettes, an example of which can be seen in the upper left corner. The manuscript is named after its last owner, Dr. Moses Gaster, a noted scholar and bibliophile who, between 1887 and 1919, acted as spiritual leader of the Spanish and Portuguese Jews' congregation in London.

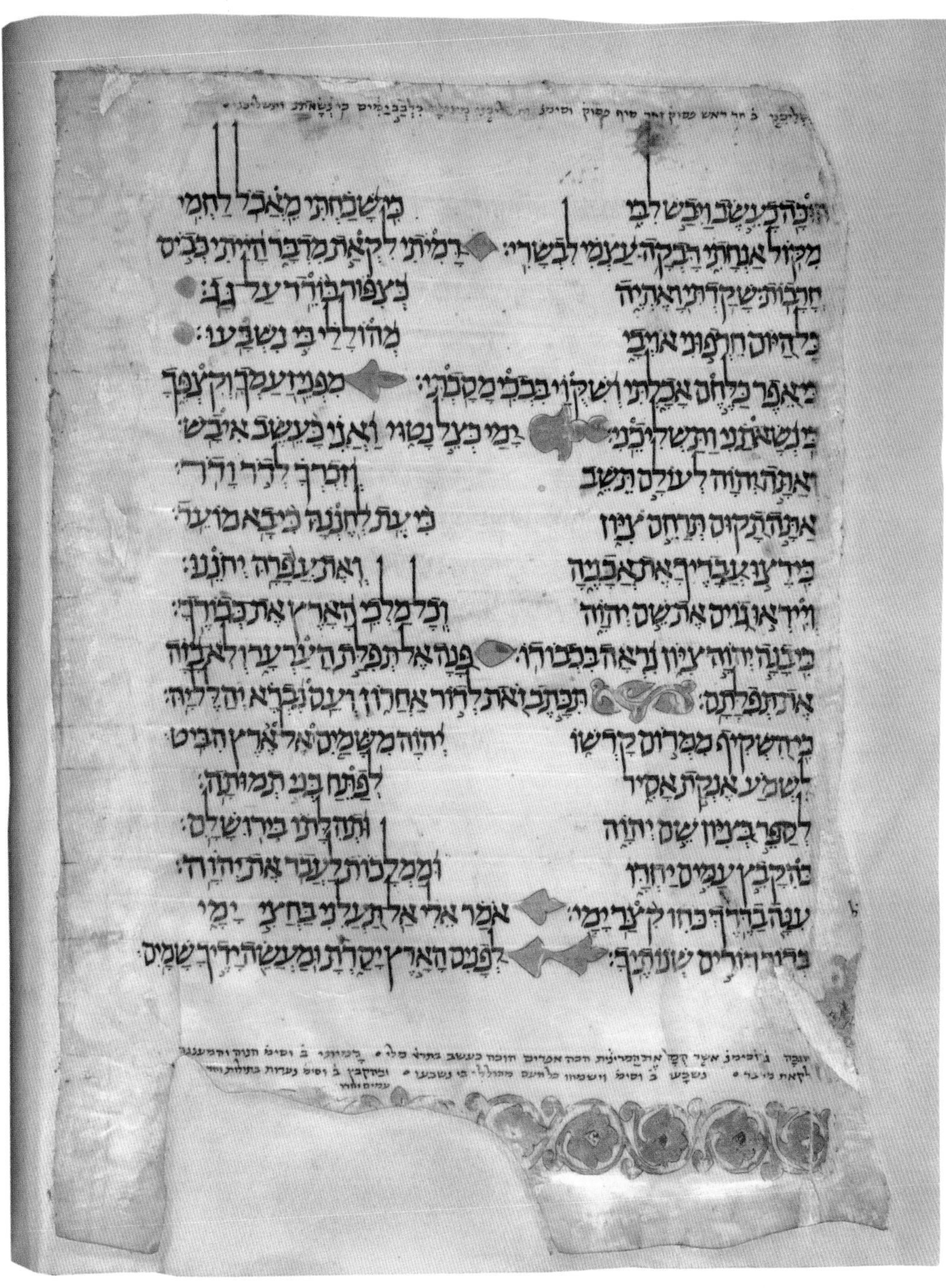

Decorated Hebrew manuscripts originating in the Islamic East (Babylonia, Egypt, Persia, Syria and Palestine) lack figurative imagery and are poor in text illustrations. Carpet pages with geometric and arabesque designs, micrography (patterned minute lettering) and divisional motifs, emphasized in Islamic illumination, typify their decoration. On this page, featuring Psalm 102, verse demarcation has been created with golden vegetal fillers. Particularly striking is the decorative golden chain below the masoretic notation in the lower margin.

6 Psalm 102 with divisional motifs
First Gaster Bible
Hagiographa
Egypt?
9th or 10th century
300 x 265 mm
MS Or. 9879, f. 23v

7 Deuteronomy 19
Second Gaster Bible
Fragments from the Pentateuch
Persia or Babylonia?
11th or 12th century
385 x 300 mm
MS Or. 9880, f. 34r

The distinctive layout of this page, boasting a gold-lined outer frame, vertical partitions, fine calligraphy and masoretic rubrics, testifies to the former glory of this manuscript, which has, unfortunately, been damaged. Probably Babylonian in origin, the fine decoration consists chiefly of dainty gilded rosettes with red centres enclosed in blue ringlets, placed either at regular intervals between the scriptural columns, or within the text to mark important sections. The floral ornamentation was inspired by Persian art.

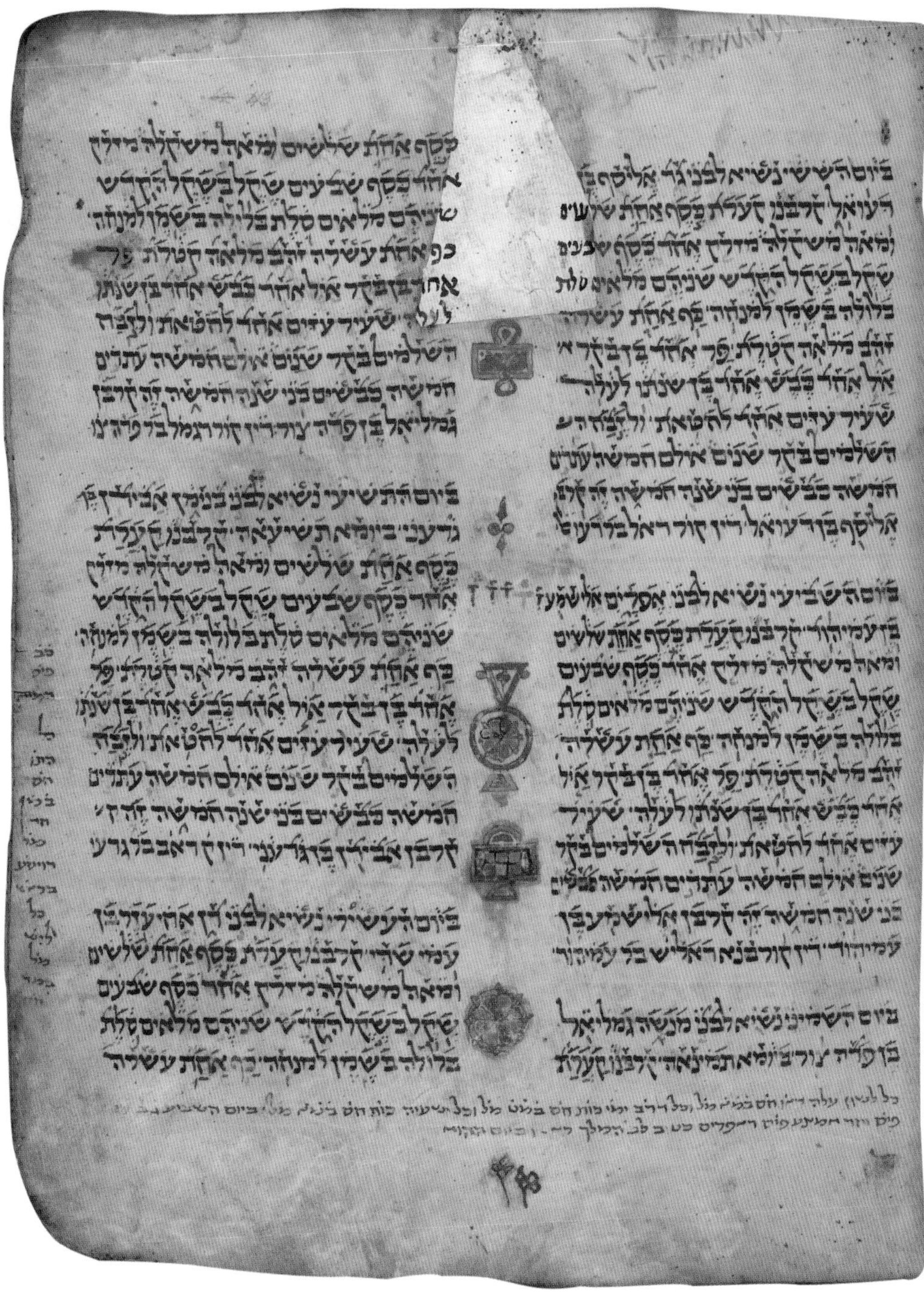

The vessels painted between the scriptural columns represent the princes' gifts to the Desert Sanctuary, as described in Numbers 7, part of which has been copied on this page. Medieval Hebrew Bibles produced in Islamic lands rarely contain text illustrations, making this an exceptionally rare specimen. Note the superlinear punctuation, with the vowel points placed above the consonantal text. This system was developed in Babylonia during the 6th and 7th centuries and was eventually superceded by the sublinear pointing that was perfected by the Tiberian Masoretes (*Masorah* scholars from Tiberias, Palestine).

8 Holy vessels
Pentateuch
Persia
c. 11th century
370 x 290 mm
MS Or. 1467, f. 43r

9–10 Micrographic carpet pages
with Psalms verses
The San'a Pentateuch
San'a, Yemen
1469
400 x 280 mm
MS Or. 2348, ff. 38v-39r

These stylized representations of fish swimming in the deep sea and mountains, outlined in scriptural micrography, contain mostly text from Psalms 119, 121 and 122. An exclusive and original form of Jewish art, micrography is the weaving of minute lettering into abstract, geometric and figurative designs. This scribal practice began around the 9th century in Egypt and Palestine and was first used in biblical codices (manuscripts copied in

book format) to pattern the masoretic notes. The colouring of the space-filled arabesques and the decorative elements in these splendid carpet pages were probably inspired by designs on contemporary metal works and enamelled glassware – crafts usually associated with the Jews of Yemen. According to scholars, both the ornamentation and the calligraphic configurations in the manuscript are the achievement of one person, the scribe.

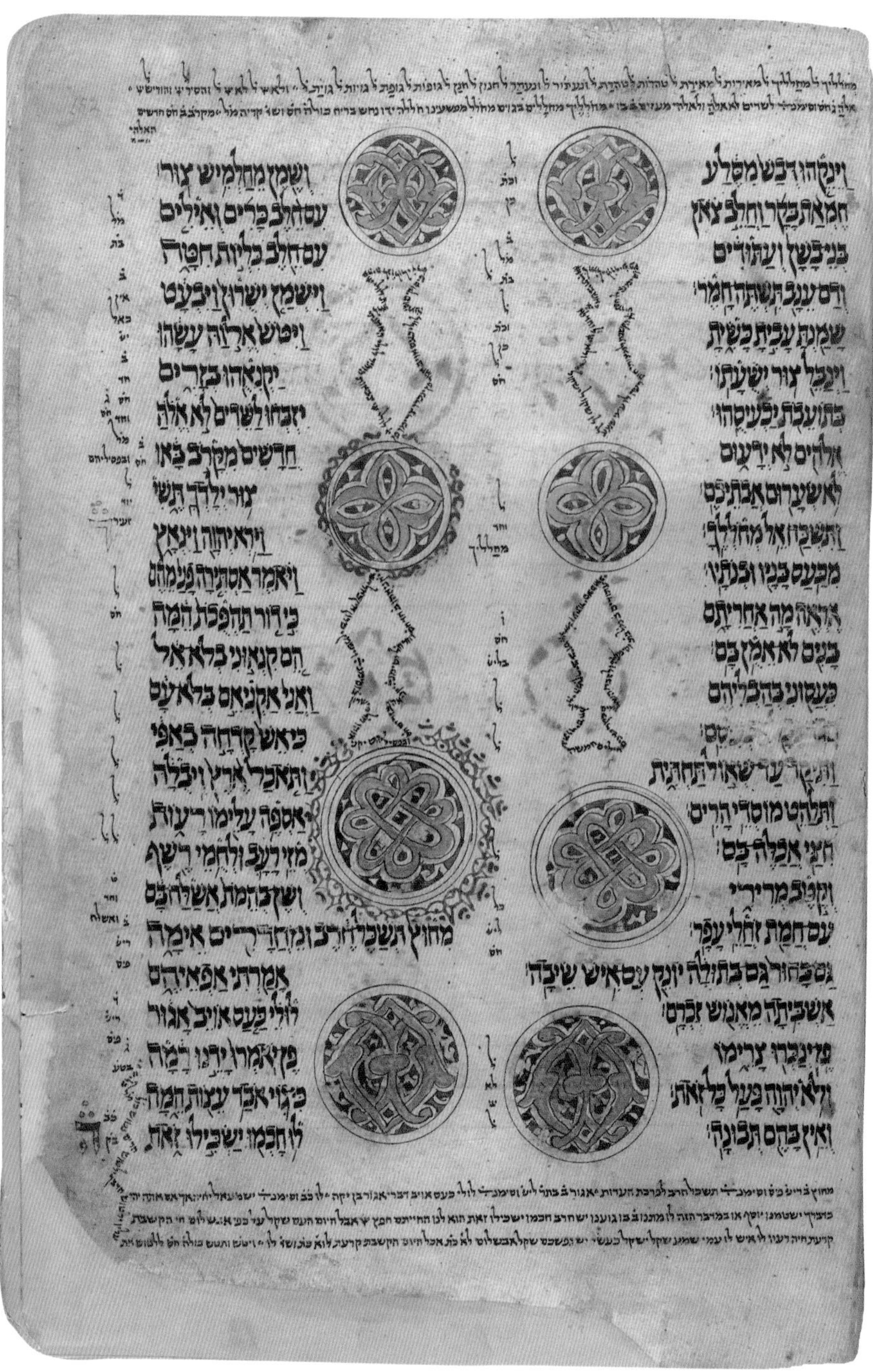

11 *Shirat Ha'azinu*, the poem 'Give Ear'
The San'a Pentateuch
San'a, Yemen
1469
400 x 280 mm
MS Or. 2348, f. 152r

Penned in two columns, in a typical Yemenite square script, is a section from *Shirat Ha'azinu* ('Give Ear'; Deuteronomy 32), the lyrical poem that Moses recited in front of the Israelites before his death. The central decoration combines characteristically Jewish elements with adapted Islamic motifs: micrographic *Masorah*, shaped in the form of fish, is interspersed with medallions filled with coloured rosettes and geometric interlacing. A corpus of complex notations aimed at preserving the Hebrew biblical text intact and safeguarding its correct transmission, the *Masorah* became a favourite medium for artistic creativity in medieval biblical handwritten books.

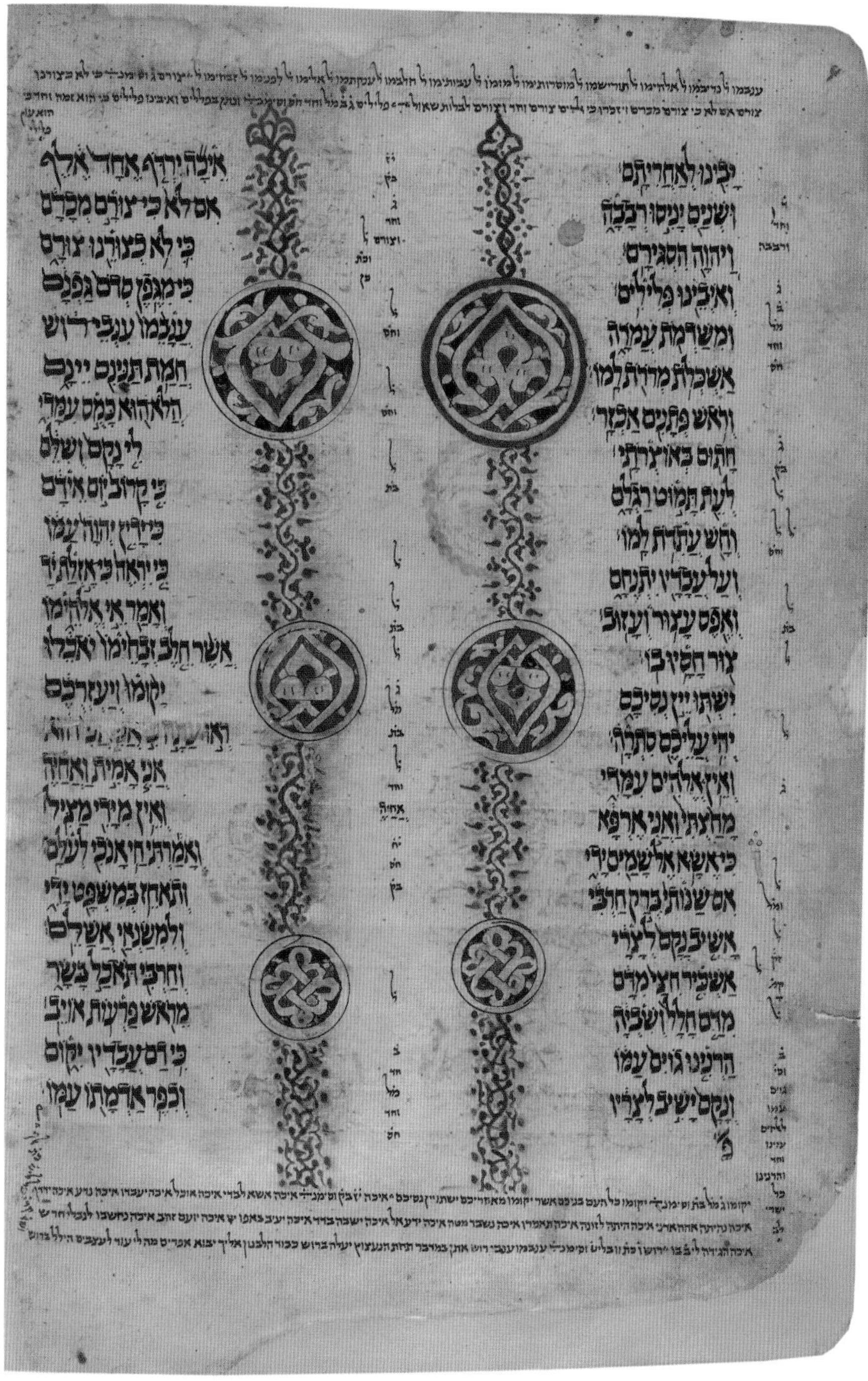

Between the columns of poetical text (*Shirat Ha'azinu*, Deuteronomy 32) are two strips of stylized knots and palmettes inspired most probably by contemporary Yemenite designs. Often used in a magical context, knot patterns were particularly common in the Muslim world, but were equally popular in medieval illuminated Hebrew codices. As in the previous opening (*fig.* 11), here, too, the decoration is functional, filling out the space between the columns of text. Particularly striking is the perfect justification – on the right and left margins – of the script on both pages.

12 *Shirat Ha'azinu*, the poem 'Give Ear'
The San'a Pentateuch
San'a, Yemen
1469
400 x 280 mm
MS Or. 2348, f. 152v

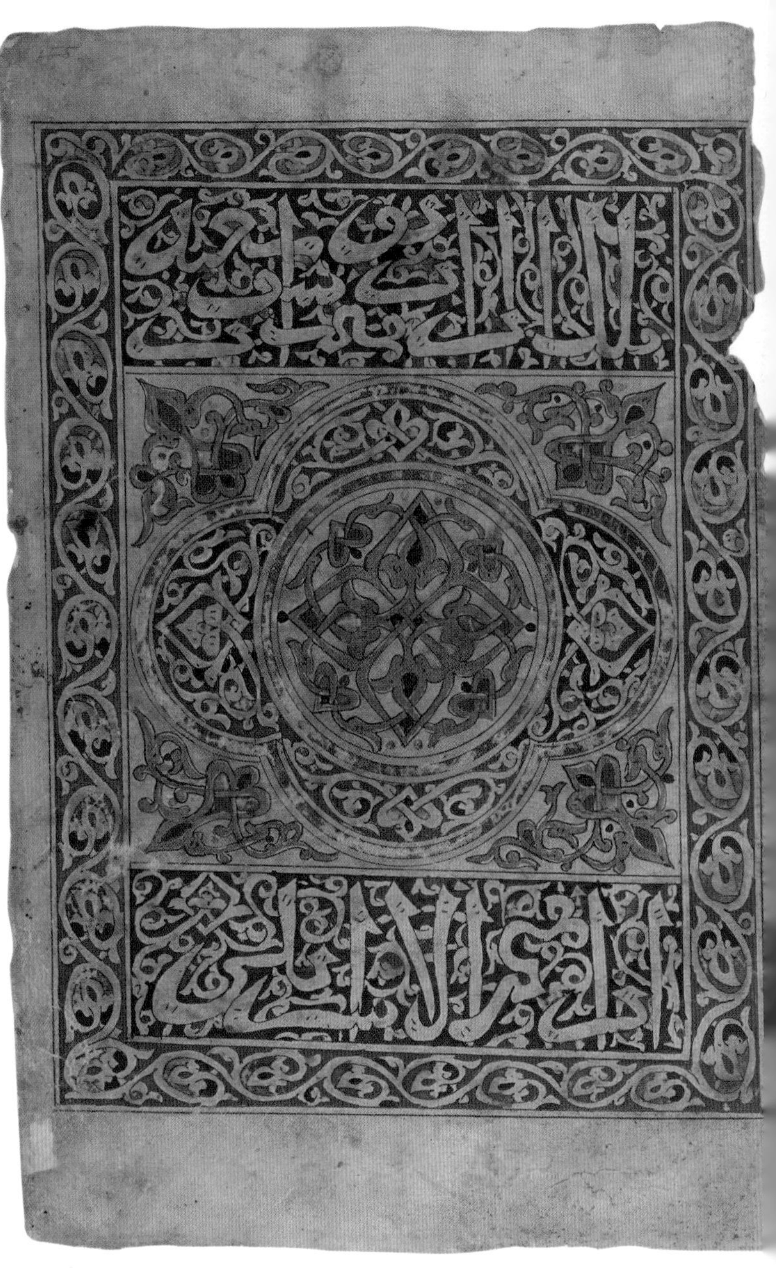

13–14 Colophon pages
The San'a Pentateuch
San'a, Yemen
1469
400 x 280 mm
MS Or. 2348, ff. 154v-155r

These splendid colophon pages, featuring Arabic calligraphy and Islamic-style floral and geometric embellishments, look strikingly Muslim. The date of the manuscript's completion is given according to the Muslim calendar: '... finished 6th Safar of the year 874' (corresponding to 15 August 1469); and the Arabic equivalent, 'Ibrahim ibn Yusuf ibn Sa'id ibn Ibrahim al-Isr'ili',

replaces the patron's Hebrew name. Although the scribe did not sign his name in the colophon, the calligraphy and layout of the manuscript evoke the style of Benayah ben Se'adyah ben Zeharyah ben Marga, a major Yemenite scribe (d. 1490) who had worked on several commissions for Abraham ben Yosef ben Sa'id ben Abraham, the patron of this Pentateuch.

15–16 Preliminary pages with patron's name
Latter Prophets
San'a, Yemen
1475
400 x 280 mm
MS Or. 2211, ff. IV-2r

The intricate arabesque frames, elaborate medallions and Arabic inscriptions, with the patron's name, conform to Islamic tradition, but the predominant floral motifs within the central roundels derive from the Chinese lotus. The latter penetrated Muslim Near East decoration after the Mongol conquest in the 13th century. The inscription records that Abraham ben Yosef ben Sa'id

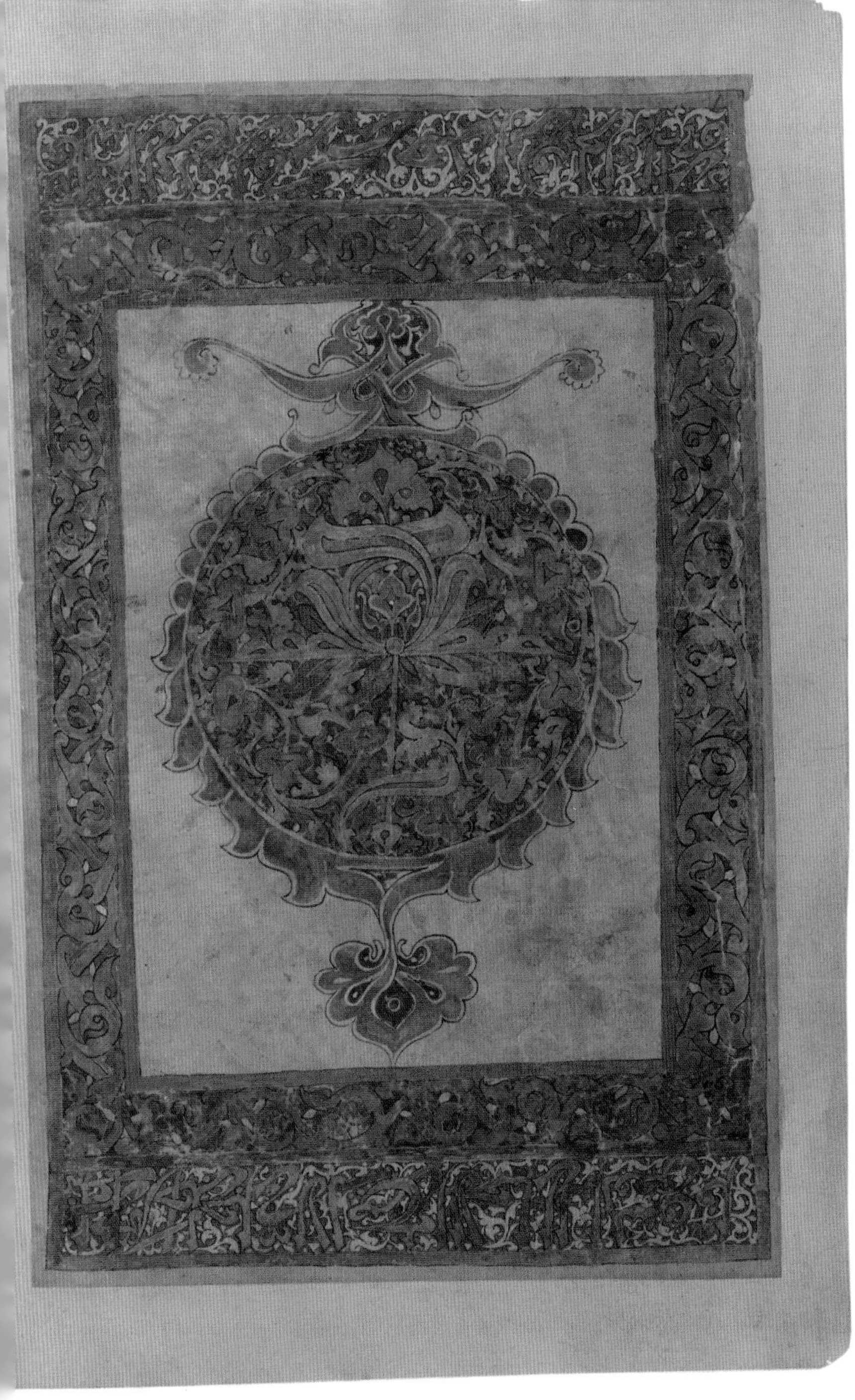

ben Abraham ordered the manuscript to be written for a synagogue in his city. The lengthy micrographic colophon on f. 320r states that the work was completed in 1475 at San'a by Benayah ben Se'adyah ben Zeharyah ben Marga for the patron named earlier. The British Library holds two other manuscripts executed by Benayah the Scribe for the same client.

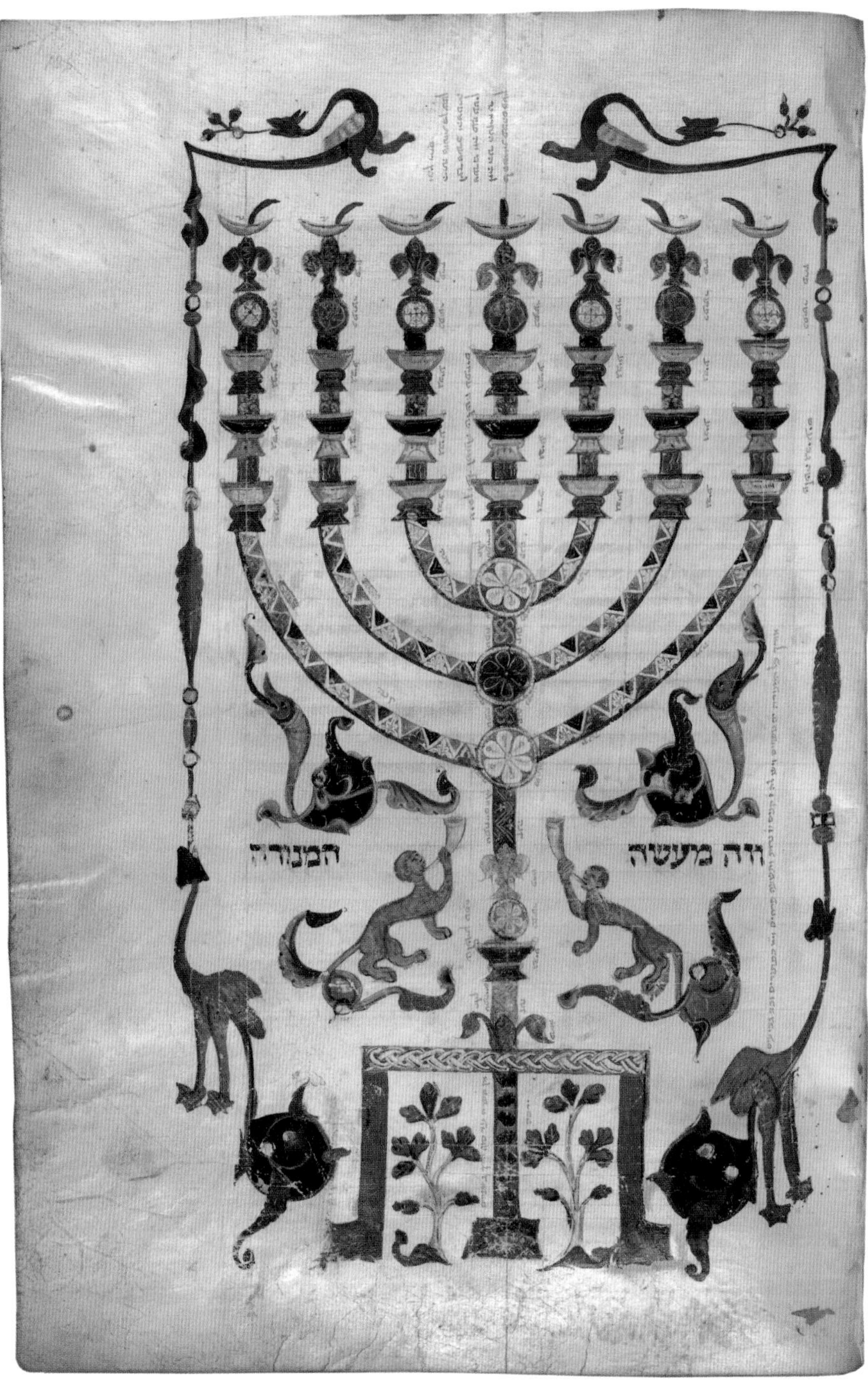

17 Seven-branched Candelabrum
Hebrew Bible in two volumes
Rome?, Italy
before 1240
390 x 260 mm
MS Harley 5710 (v.1), f. 136r

In this opening, the *Menorah*, or seven-branched candelabrum, has been finely painted with its traditional knops, flowers, candles and tripod support. Surrounding the *Menorah* on the vellum ground are dragons, hybrids, and fantastic animals. One of the oldest Jewish symbols, the *Menorah* was crafted by Bezalel for the desert Tabernacle (Exodus 37:17-24). Its earliest representation in a Hebrew manuscript is apparently found in a Near Eastern 10th-century Bible. This miniature comes from a two-volume Hebrew Bible (see also *fig.*18) formerly held in the collection of Robert and Edward Harley, Earls of Oxford and Mortimer.

The main panel in this opening is composed of two blue medallions inhabited by red-crested cockerels separated by a vegetal motif. Beneath it, on a blue and red filigree ground, is the opening word *Mishle* (Proverbs). The outer frame is decorated with grotesques. The decoration is typical of the region and period, with predominantly blue, grey and brownish serrated leaves, living creatures and fantastic beasts. This highly important codex was sold in 1240, proving that the manuscript was completed at an earlier date. The censorial notes of Clemento Renatto (V.1, f. 258v) and Domenico Fresolo (V.2, f. 301v) confirm that the codex remained in Italy until at least the 16th century.

18 Opening to Proverbs
Hebrew Bible in two volumes
Rome?, Italy
before 1240
390 x 260 mm
MS Harley 5711, (V.2), f. 241v

19 Opening to Jeremiah
Former and Latter Prophets
Italy?
14th century
240 x 380 mm
MS Add. 11657, f. 213r

The first word of Jeremiah, *Divre* ('The words of'), is inscribed in an embellished rectangular panel with lateral and marginal foliage ornamentation in rich shades of pink, red, green and dazzling blue – the predominant hue. The elegant decoration, enhanced with gold leaf inlays, evokes an Italianate style. Although Meshulam the Scribe penned the Hebrew biblical text in a characteristic German hand, the manuscript's structure – quires of five sheets each – suggests an Italian origin. Migrant Jewish copyists often preserved their native calligraphic styles while endorsing methods and practices prevalent in their new surroundings.

This codex presents a beautifully written Ashkenazi square script and abounds in finely illuminated first word panels and borders placed at the start of the prophetical books. The attractive panel on this leaf has ornate blue and red grounds filled with feathery scrolls and gold enhancements. Stemming from it are two embellished extensions composed of colourful vegetal elements, a long-beaked bird and gilded dots. The panel inscription spelling *Devar* ('The word of') opens the prophetical Book of Joel.

20 Opening to Joel
Former and Latter Prophets
Italy
14th century
240 x 380 mm
MS Add. 11657, f. 318v

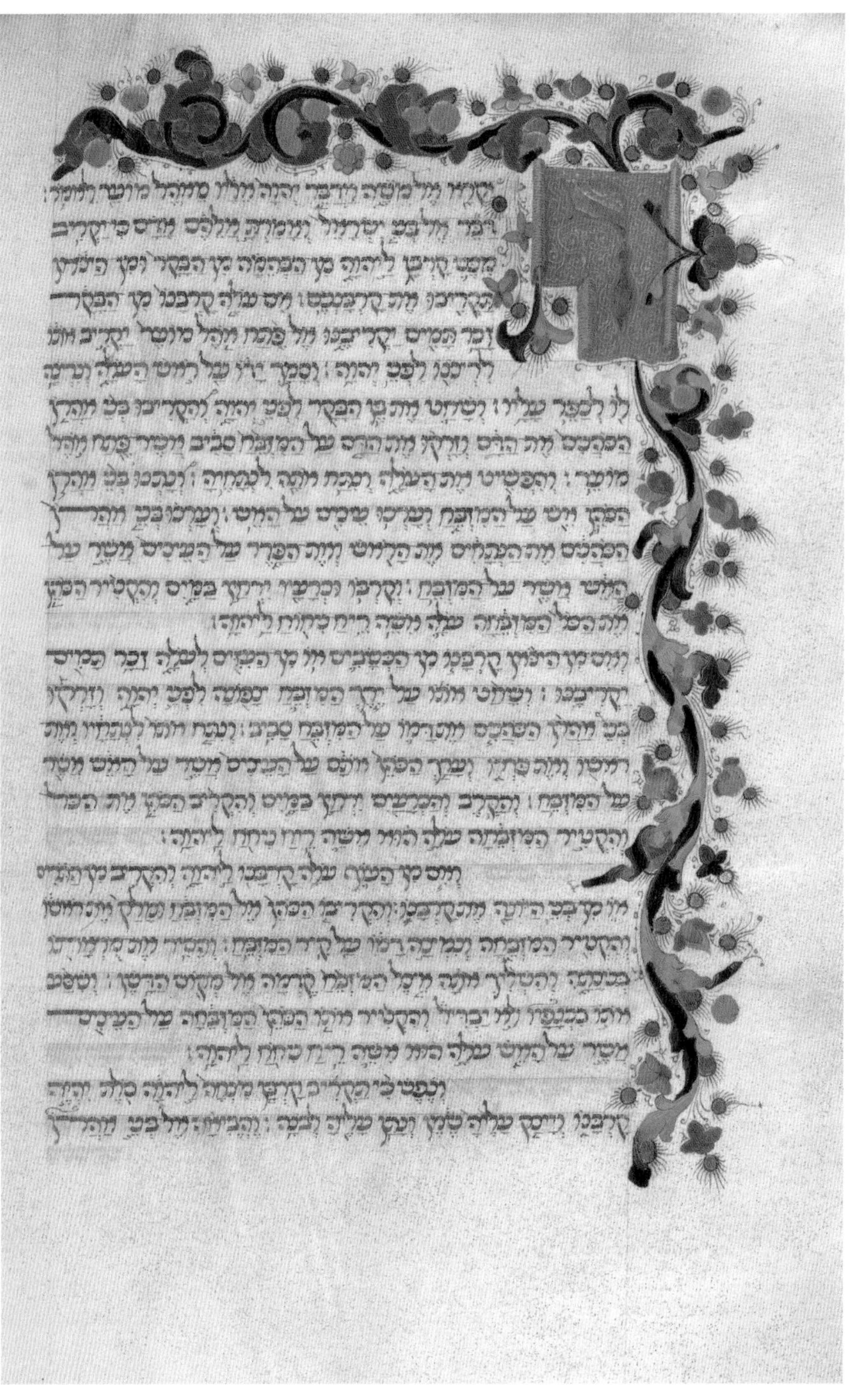

21 Opening to Leviticus
The Duke of Sussex's Italian Pentateuch
Italy
14th or 15th century
335 x 225 mm
MS Add. 15423, f. 65v

Illuminated letters, a trait usually associated with Latin manuscripts, is rarely encountered in Hebrew illuminated hand-made books; however, in this Pentateuch, embellished letters replace the habitual decorated first words. Within a green ornate panel, in the form of an unfurling scroll, is the letter *Vav*, moulded in burnished gold. The beautified wreaths adorning the page display undulating acanthus leaves and florid sprigs strewn with golden dots. The manuscript's last owner was Augustus Frederick, Duke of Sussex (1773–1843), sixth son of King George III.

The opening to Deuteronomy is marked by a pink scroll-shaped panel inhabited by the initial letter *Alef*, painted in gold. Flanking the text on two sides are floral garlands and luxuriant foliage in vibrant colours enhanced with gilded inlays. The scriptural text was penned in a vocalized (with added vowels), semi-cursive, Hebrew handwriting, whose dominant rotundity closely resembles Italian Latin scripts, particularly the Carolingian style.

22 Opening to Deuteronomy
The Duke of Sussex's Italian Pentateuch
Italy
14th or 15th century
335 x 225 mm
MS Add. 15423, f. 117r

23–24 'The Song of the Sea', Exodus 15
The Duke of Sussex's Italian Bible
Ferrara?, Italy
1448
245 x 180 mm
MS Add. 15251, ff. 49v-50r

Sung by the Israelites after the miraculous Red Sea crossing, the script of this epic hymn has traditionally been laid out on these pages in the form of 'bricks', a practice going back to Talmudic times and still in use today. The sumptuous gold leaf border with stylized florid motifs and animal medallions, particularly those featuring deer, point to a Ferrarese illuminator.

His identity, however, is not revealed in the colophon or elsewhere in the codex. The Duke of Sussex (1773–1843), who owned the manuscript until its sale in 1844, was known for his keen interest in biblical studies and Hebrew. His 50,000-volume library included ancient Hebrew manuscripts and printed books, many of which now form part of the British Library collection.

25 Opening to Isaiah
The Duke of Sussex's Italian Bible
Ferrara?, Italy
1448
245 x 180 mm
MS Add. 15251, f. 216v

Many of the initial word panels in this Bible are subdivided into distinct compartments, as seen here. In the right-hand chamber, the word *Hazon* (Vision, Isaiah 1:1) is penned on a tricolour surface of deep blue, green and pink. Floral and abstract designs, arranged symmetrically on penwork grounds, as seen in the left and upper compartments, were apparently common in Ferrarese illumination.

Between the two decorative panels above, filled with brightly coloured flowers and spiral shells, the deep blue panel at the centre is inscribed in gold with the opening word of Chronicles 1:1: *Adam* (Man). The text columns are bordered by masoretic annotations, which in the lower margin form micrographic semi-circles. This codex belonged to the Royal Hebraist, the Duke of Sussex, on whose death it was sold to the British Museum.

26 Opening to Chronicles
The Duke of Sussex's Italian Bible
Ferrara?, Italy
1448
245 x 180 mm
MS Add. 15251, f. 313v

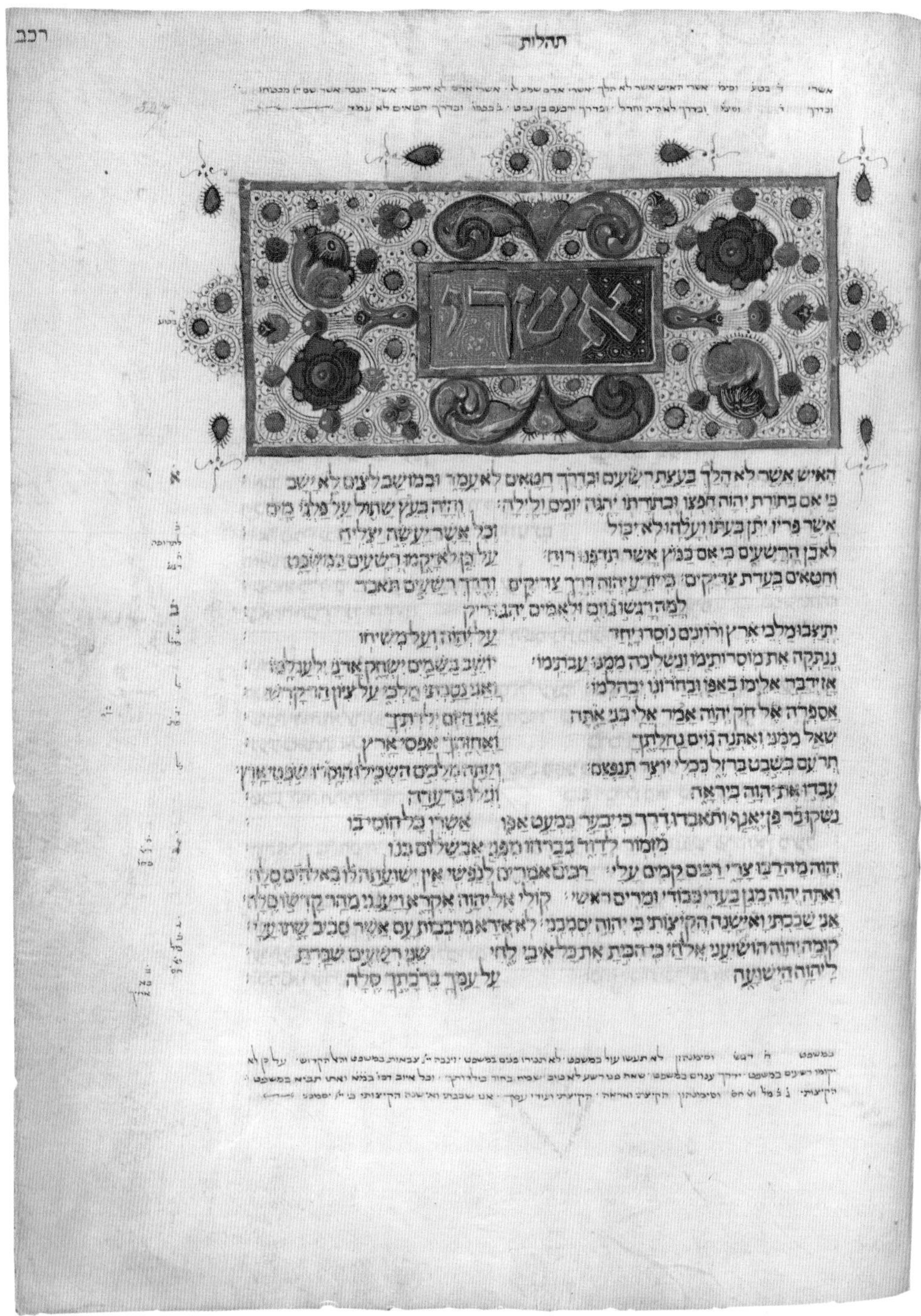

27 Opening to Psalms
The Duke of Sussex's Italian Bible
Ferrara?, Italy
1448
245 x 180 mm
MS Add. 15251, f. 347r

The elaborate initial word panel above shows a high level of skill and refinement. Although the colophon lacks the artist's name or the place where the manuscript was completed, the illuminations were most probably executed in Ferrara. The Spanish-Jewish scribe Moses Akrish, who penned the text, had settled and worked in Ferrara, where he produced most of his manuscripts, seven of which survive. He probably entrusted the decorations to a local Christian workshop.

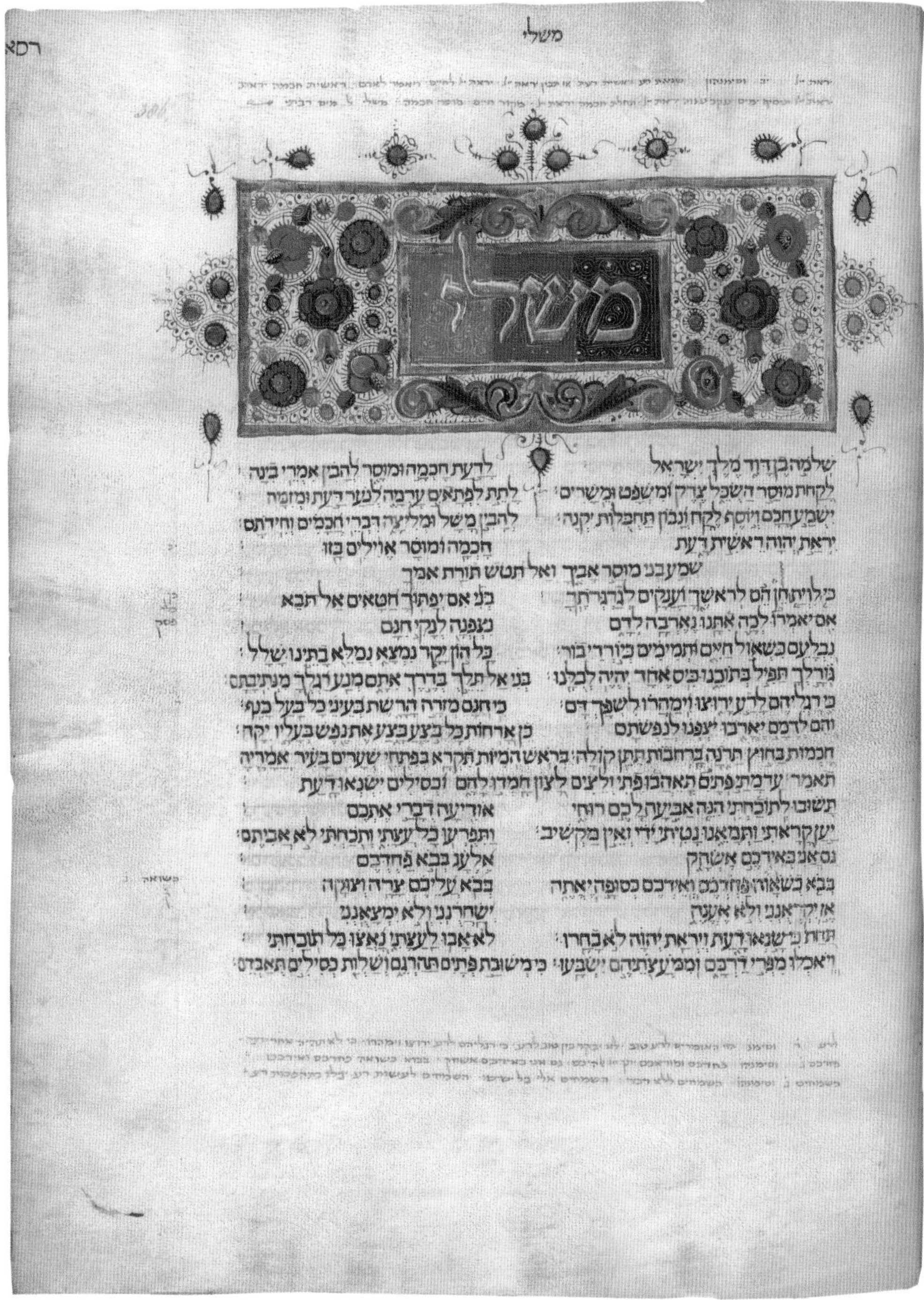

This elegant introductory panel, inscribed with the word *Mishle* (Proverbs), is filled with large open flowers and a filigree ornamental background, which characterize contemporary Ferrarese illumination. Moses Akrish (*fig.* 27) copied the text in a Sephardi square hand, but used quires (gatherings) of five sheets each, a practice associated with Hebrew manuscript production in northern Italy. This clearly illustrates how immigrant Jewish copyists often retained their indigenous handwriting while fostering local techniques.

28 Beginning of Proverbs
The Duke of Sussex's Italian Bible
Ferrara?, Italy
1448
245 x 180 mm
MS Add. 15251, f. 386r

29 King Solomon
The Coburg Pentateuch
Coburg, Germany
1395
290 x 220 mm
MS Add. 19776, f. 54v (detail)

King Solomon, famed for his wisdom, justice and his remarkable ability to converse with the animal kingdom, is shown in this miniature seated on a throne shaped like the roof of a building. The dog, winged dragon and lion at his feet illustrate the legend that Solomon's throne was guarded by animals who helped the king climb its steps. The scroll unfurled on the right contains micrographic designs; the other scroll, held by Solomon, is amusingly chained to the dog's neck. Dragon and scroll motifs, which abound in this codex, were apparently quite popular in Germany at the time, in both Latin and Hebrew manuscripts.

Exhibited here is the opening to Numbers, which describes the organization of the 12 tribes of Israel into four camps, each with its own banner. This miniature depicts four soldiers in booths, each soldier holding standards bearing devices traditionally associated with the leading tribes: a lion for Judah, a bull for Joseph, a serpent for Dan and an eagle for Reuben. The illuminated initial word spells *Va-Yedaber* (and He spoke), a reference to the Lord speaking to Moses, as found in the first verse of Numbers. It is unlikely that Hayim, the scribe in charge of copying the text, executed the striking miniatures in this codex.

30 Opening to Numbers
The Duke of Sussex's German Pentateuch
Germany
c. 1300
230 x 165 mm
MS Add. 15282, f. 179v

31 Opening to Deuteronomy
The Duke of Sussex's German Pentateuch
Germany
c. 1300
230 x 165 mm
MS Add. 15282, f. 238r

The embellished word *Eleh* ('These are the words') in the central blue panel refers to Moses' address to the Israelites, as indicated in the opening verse of Deuteronomy. The elaborate architectural framework, with Gothic-style lancet windows, straight-sided gables and pinnacle forms, is reminiscent of contemporary German church edifices. The elephant painted inside the golden Shield of David (hexagram) was probably modelled on images found in Latin bestiaries. In the medieval period the hexagram or Seal of Solomon, was not, as nowadays, a distinctly Judaic emblem, but served as a magical symbol in both Christianity and Islam.

Although the figure playing the harp in the ornamented panel is King David, one would normally expect to see here a portrait of King Solomon, to whom Ecclesiastes is traditionally ascribed. Manifest throughout the manuscript is the pronounced south German style of illumination. Strongly contrasting colours, Gothic architectural elements, odd-looking human faces and exaggerated grotesque dragons are just some of the traits defining this style. Owned by the Duke of Sussex in the 19th century, the manuscript may have been in Italian ownership several centuries earlier, as its 16th-century gold-tooled Venetian binding appears to indicate.

32 Opening to Ecclesiastes
The Duke of Sussex's German Pentateuch
Germany
c. 1300
230 x 165 mm
MS Add. 15282, f. 302r

33–34 Differences in Hagiographa
Hebrew Bible with *Masorah*
Franco-German hand
c. 14th century
265 x 195 mm
MS Or. 4227, ff. 199v-200r

Apart from some crudely decorated headings and coloured pericope markers, the only illuminated elements in this codex are the lists displayed beneath the arched arcades, seen here. The lists show differences between Eastern and Western recensions (critical revisions) in the books of the Hagiographa or Writings, which is the third major division of the Hebrew Bible. The columns of the arcades are each divided into two separate sections, and filled with fretwork, scroll and foliate designs executed in gold on coloured grounds.

Other distinctive elements featured in the decoration include animal medallions, architectural dividers and gargoyle motifs, as seen at the base of the columns on the right-hand page. Similar decorative arcades enclosing massoretic lists (the 613 Jewish precepts, or liturgical calendars) can be found in a number of 14th-century Hebrew Bibles produced in Spain. Comparable examples are the decorated Canon Tables in Gospel books, which might have served as models.

35 Biblical readings for Passover
Catalonia, Spain
c. 1350–75
256 x 192 mm
MS Or. 1424, f. 3v

This manuscript comprises biblical readings and liturgical poems recited in the synagogue during Passover. Texts such as these were sometimes bound together with the *Hagadah*, and sometimes, as in the case here, bound separately. The unidentified illuminator has made lavish use of burnished gold in all 11 initial word panels found in the manuscript. He additionally endowed them with coloured tooled surfaces and marginal decorations, as seen here. The bearded head donning a high hat and the foliage pattern extending beneath the panel are particularly attractive.

This dedicatory frontispiece is composed of a word panel, a diapered carpet and various inscriptions. In the dark blue panel dwells the word *Mikdashyah* (Lord's Temple), penned in gold letters. Note the letter *kof*, whose extended vertical stroke ends in a *fleur-de-lis*. A floral scroll pattern in red and violet penwork adorns the carpet area. The central inscription states that the original patron, Isaac the son of Judah of Tulusa (Toulouse?), dedicated this *Mikdashyah* (denoting Bible) probably to a synagogue. Scriptural verses from Psalms 72, 97, 119:1 and Proverbs 3:16 border the page.

36 The Lord's Temple
The King's Bible
Hebrew Bible with *Masorah*
Solsona, Catalonia, Spain
1384
340 x 260 mm
MS Kings I, f. 2v

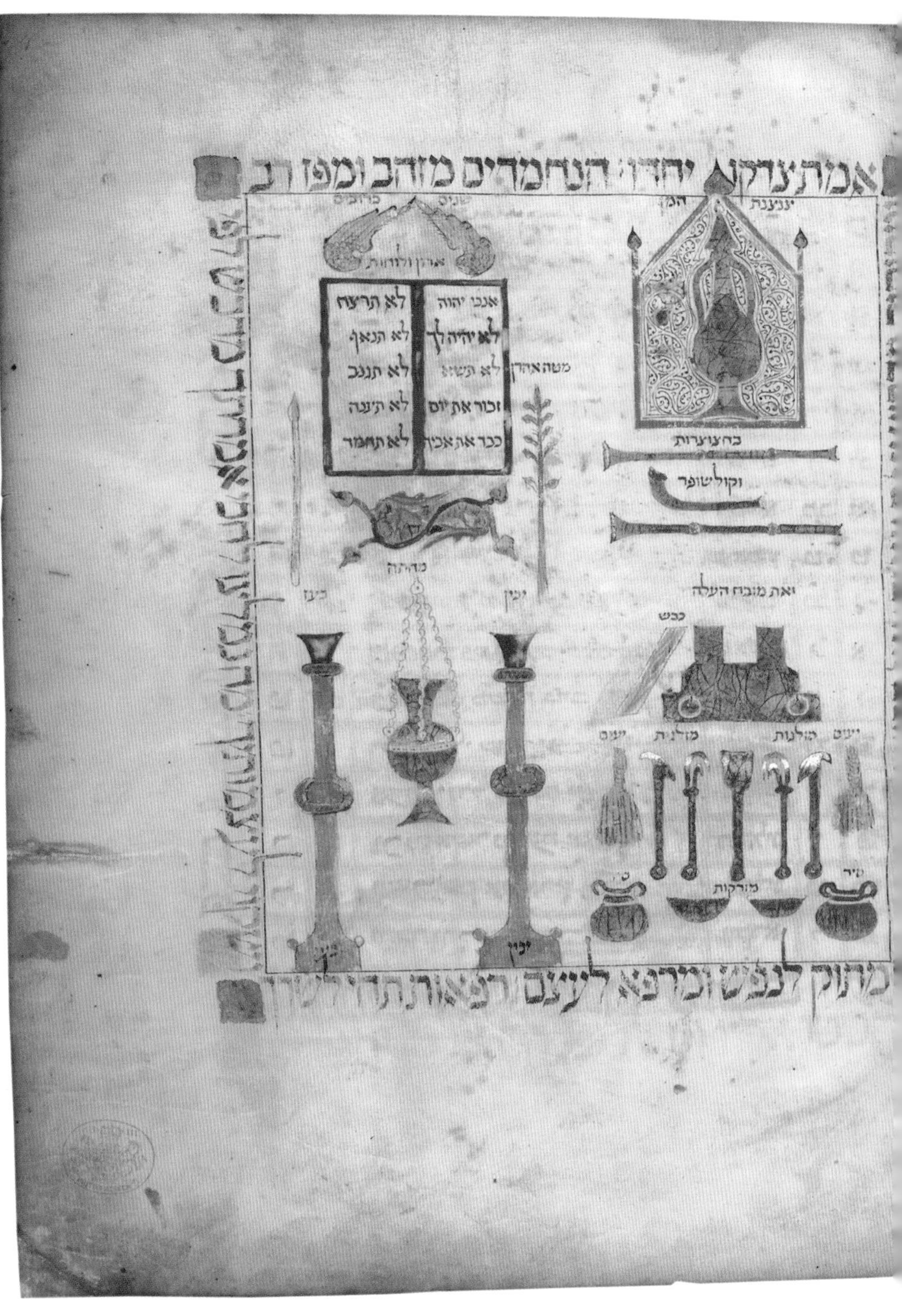

37–38 The Temple objects
The King's Bible
Hebrew Bible with *Masorah*
Solsona, Catalonia, Spain
1384
340 x 260 mm
MS King's I, ff. 3v-4r

Individually labelled, the holy objects of the Temple and the Mount of Olives opposite (lower right) are painted in pastel colours and gold on a vellum ground. Known as *Mikdashyah* (Lord's Sanctuary), the Hebrew Bible was regarded by Spanish Jews as a substitute for the destroyed Temple in Jerusalem; thus depictions of its utensils and the Mount of Olives conveyed the traditional Jewish longing to rebuild the Temple in Messianic times. The

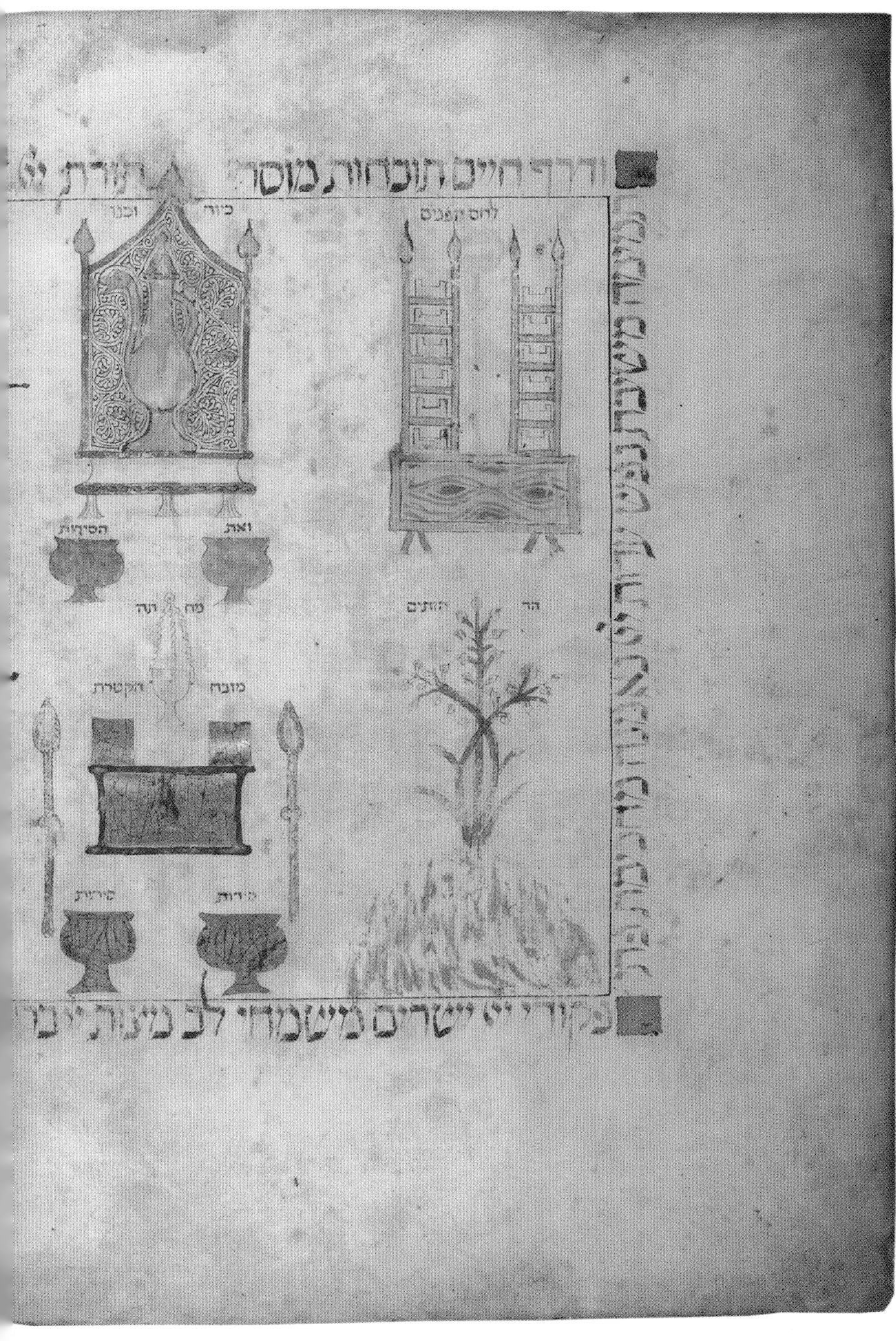

codex was written by Jacob, son of Joseph Ripoll for Isaac, son of Judah of Tulusa (Toulouse?), and completed in 1384 in Solsona. The Bible once belonged to a synagogue in Jerusalem, but due to Turkish persecution it was taken to Aleppo, where Laurentius d'Avrieux, Consul for France and Holland, acquired it in 1683. Known as the King's Bible, it was the only Hebrew manuscript in the collection donated to the British Museum by King George IV in 1823.

39–40 The Temple utensils
The Duke of Sussex's Catalan Bible
Hebrew Bible with *Masorah*
Catalonia, Spain
third quarter of 14th century
357 x 285 mm
MS Add. 15250, ff. 3v-4r

Executed in burnished gold, the sacred objects seen here are a combination of the contents of the Desert Sanctuary, the Solomonic and Herodian temples and the future Messianic Temple, as described in scriptural and rabbinic sources. Most prominent among the Temple utensils is the *Menorah*, the seven-branched candelabrum (opposite), one of the oldest symbols of the Jewish faith. The cleft hillock topped by a tree (above, bottom left), represents the Mount of Olives, which in Judaism is the traditional site for Messianic redemption at the end of days. The Gothic style of decoration of this codex

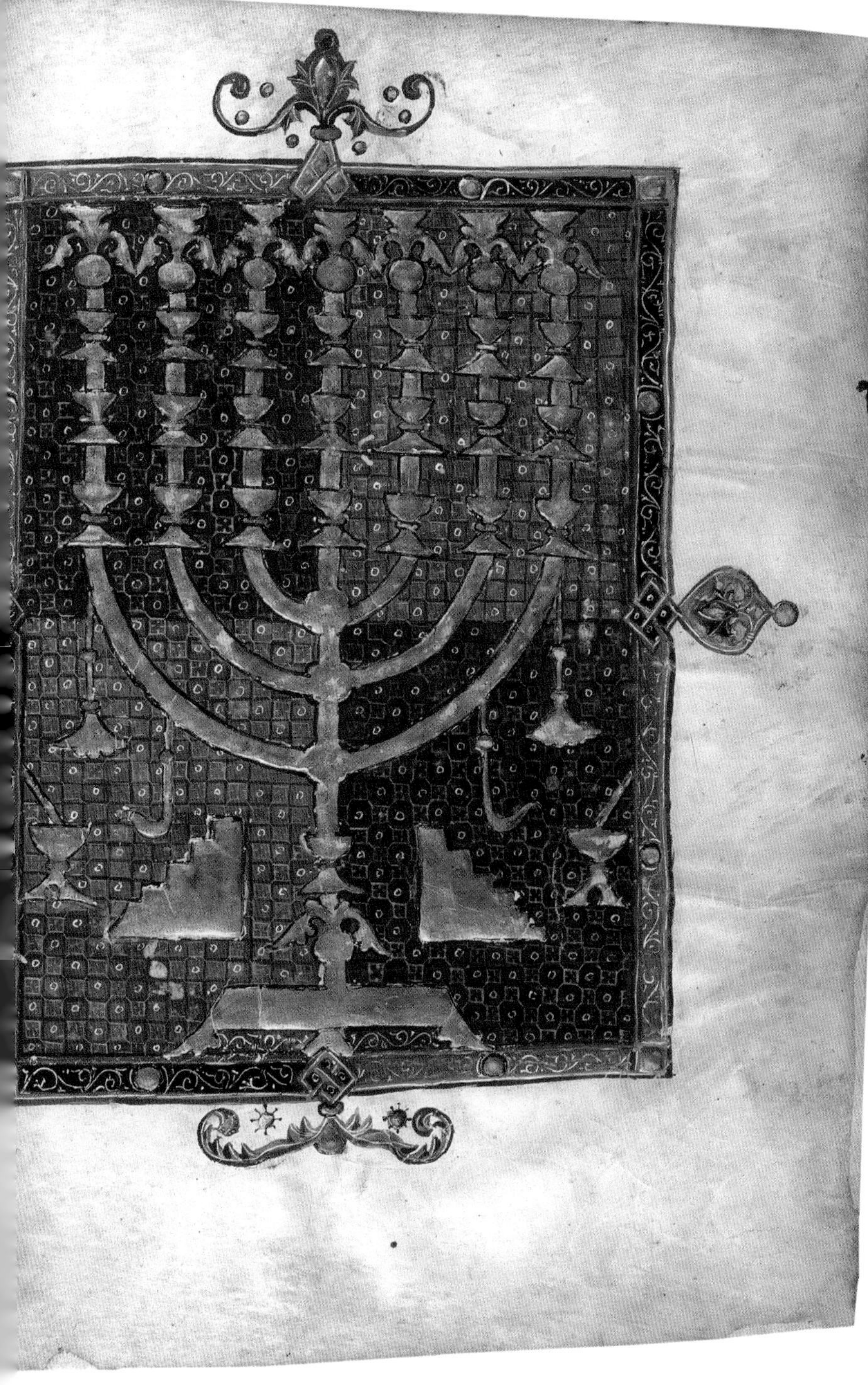

is very similar to that of the Harley Catalan Bible (*figs.* 41–2), suggesting that they were both created in the same workshop, or perhaps shared a common model. Particularly attractive are the foliate marginal extensions (top and bottom) and the palmette motifs (far left and right), which evoke elements of the Islamic artistic tradition. This manuscript was one of six biblical manuscripts acquired by the British Museum at the celebrated sale in 1844 of the library of the Duke of Sussex, brother of King George IV.

41–42 The Sanctuary implements
The Harley Catalan Bible
Hebrew Bible with *Masorah*
Catalonia, Spain
c. 1350
350 x 270 mm
MS Harley 1528, ff. 7v-8r

As in the previous opening (*figs.* 39–40), here, too, the richly illuminated selection of the Temple's holy vessels is painted on embellished blue and magenta grounds. The objects on the left-hand carpet page are captioned in ink on the gold, while on the facing page, the opening words of the Ten Commandments are inscribed on the stone-coloured tablets. The stylized Mount of Olives in the left lower corner alludes to Zechariah's Messianic prophecy (Zechariah 14 :4). The eschatological (Messianic) imagery found in

these Bibles crystallized in Spain in the 13th century and had no apparent antecedent in Christian and Jewish art. Two censorial notes signed by D. Jac. Giraldini in 1555 and Luigi da Bologna in 1602 indicate that the codex must have reached Italy before 1555. Its last owners were Robert and Edward Harley, First and Second Earls of Oxford and Mortimer, whose famed manuscript collection was sold to the British Museum in 1753. The Harley manuscripts now form part of the British Library collection.

43 List of Commandments
The Lisbon Bible
Hebrew Bible in three volumes
Lisbon, Portugal
1482
295 x 245 mm
MS Or. 2626 (v. 1), f. 13v

This page belongs to a lavishly decorated prefatory section listing the 613 *Torah* Commandments that Jews are required to keep. The *Torah*, known also as the Pentateuch, is the most sacred part of the Hebrew Bible. Among the Commandments penned on the page, some deal with the treatment of slaves. The exquisite floral and filigree ornamentation and monumental gold lettering that earned the Lisbon Bible its fame are aptly demonstrated in this opening. Samuel ben Samuel Ibn Musa copied the biblical text in an elegant square Sephardi hand for the manuscript's patron Yosef ben Yehudah al-Hakim. The sumptuous decorations were created by a team of skilled artists.

The opening of this Torah portion, which deals with the lineage of Isaac, the Patriarch Abraham's son (Genesis 25:19–28:9), is indicated by an elegant gilded marker containing the abbreviated word *parashah* (portion). This functional device is incorporated in an elongated feature embellished with feathery branches interspersed with flowers, red acorns and coloured dots. Functional decorations were first used in early Hebrew Bibles copied in the Islamic East.

44 The pericope *Toldot Yitshak* (the Generations of Isaac)
The Lisbon Bible
Hebrew Bible in three volumes
Lisbon, Portugal
1482
295 x 245 mm
MS Or. 2626 (v.1), f. 40r

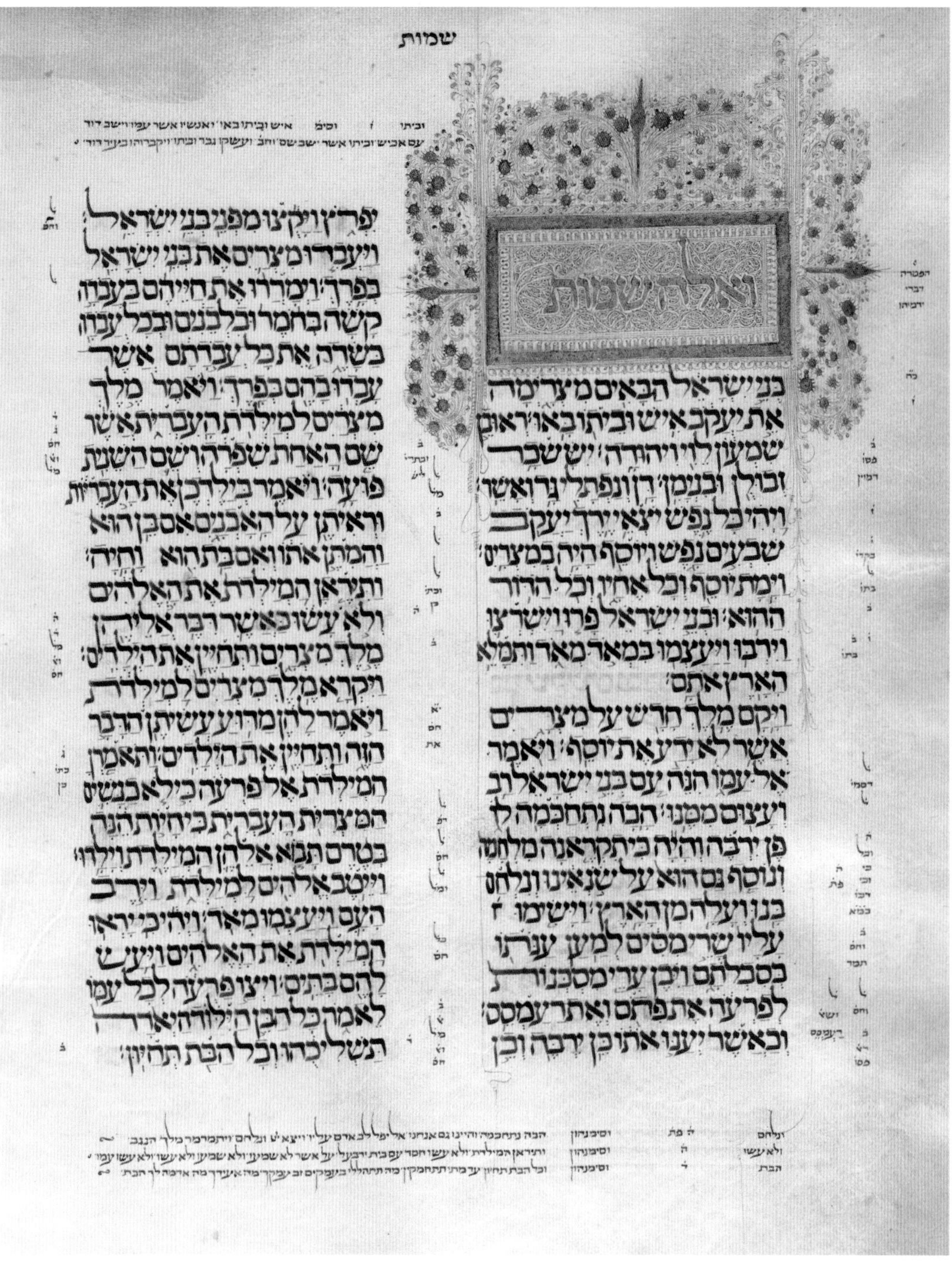

45 Opening to Exodus
The Lisbon Bible
Hebrew Bible in three volumes
Lisbon, Portugal
1482
295 x 245 mm
MS Or. 2626 (v.1), f. 61 v

This embellished opening comprises a dainty filigree panel surrounded by a flurry of mauve penwork strewn with golden dots and pistils. Two plumes resembling water fountains complete the composition. Inside the panel, penned in gold, are the opening words of Exodus *Ve-eleh shemot* ('These are the names...'). Samuel the Scribe copied the sacred text in two columns in his distinct Sephardi hand. A second, unnamed scribe, who was probably Samuel's closest collaborator, penned the massoretic notes in the margins and between the columns of text.

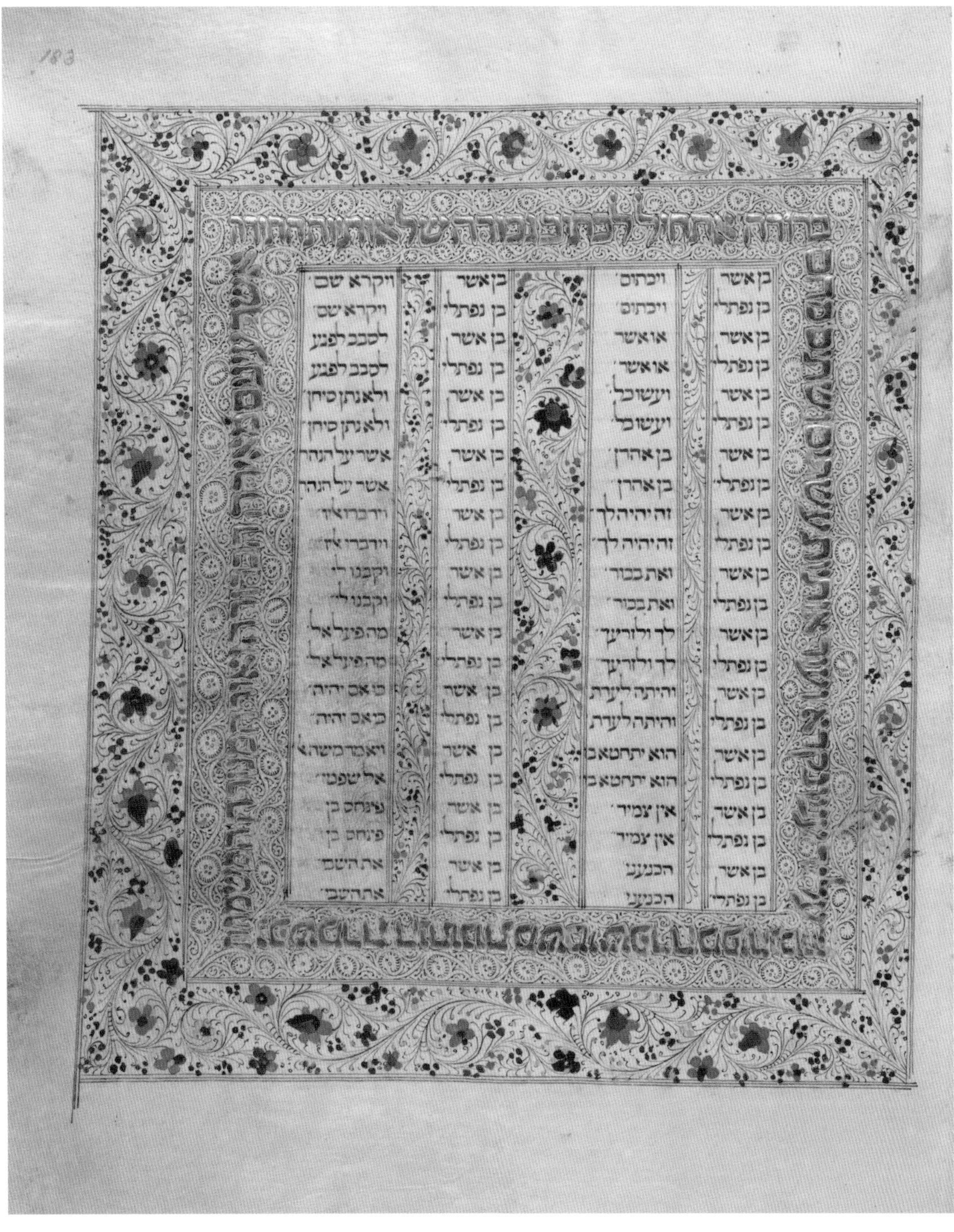

This page lists variations on the spelling of the scriptural text between the two leading 10th-century Tiberian Masoretes, Aaron Ben Asher and Moses Ben Naphtali. But since the vowels and accents were unfortunately omitted, it is impossible to see the actual differences between the two authorities. The striking mounts surrounding the lists, decorated with floral motifs, exquisite filigree penwork and gold script, are the hallmark components of the Lisbon Bible, which is regarded as the most accomplished dated codex of the Portuguese school of Hebrew illumination.

46 Differences between Ben Asher and Ben Naphtali
The Lisbon Bible
Hebrew Bible in three volumes
Lisbon, Portugal
1482
295 x 245 mm
MS Or. 2626 (v.1), f. 183r

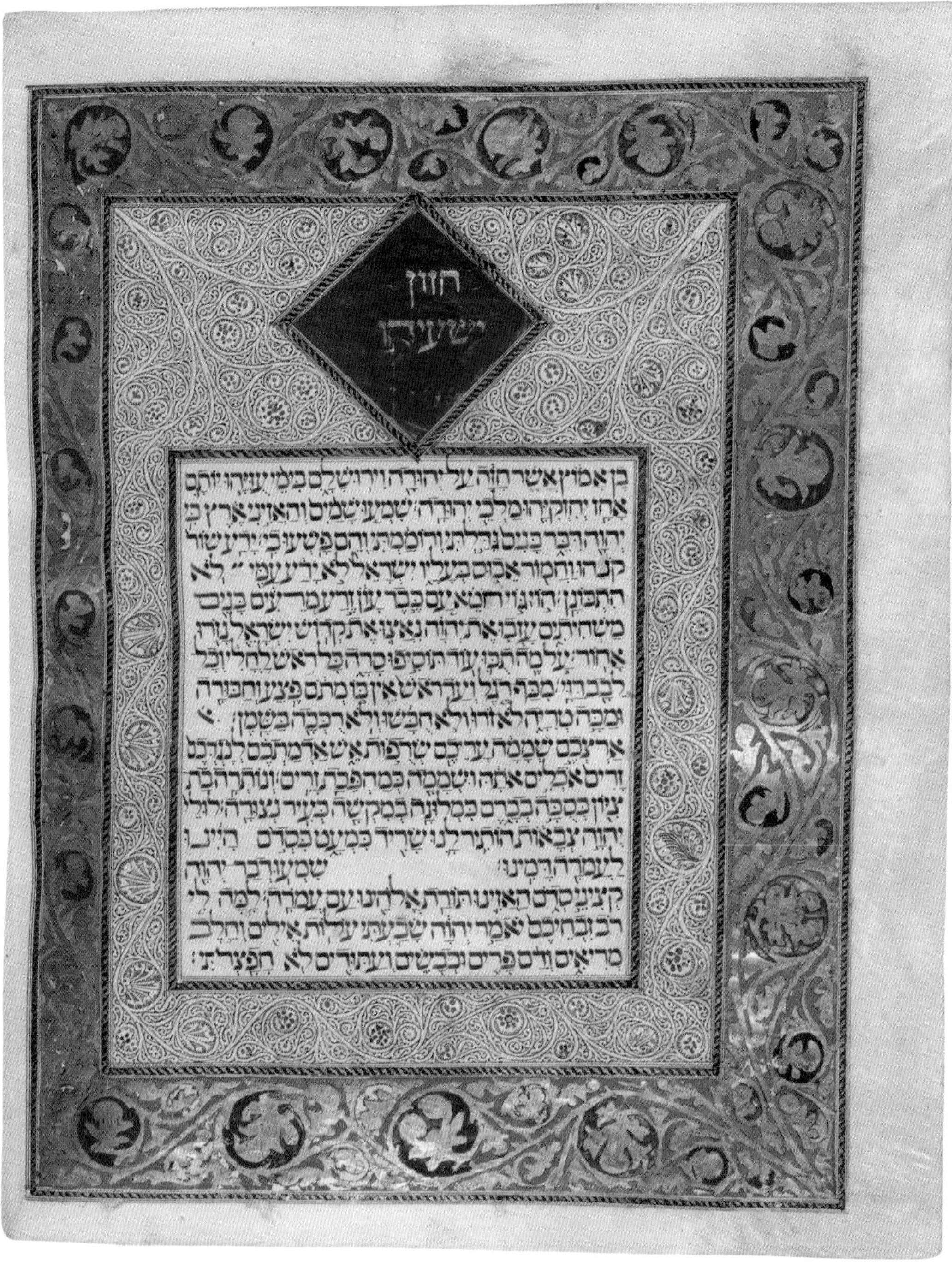

47 Opening to Isaiah
The Lisbon Bible
Hebrew Bible in three volumes
Lisbon, Portugal
1482
295 x 245 mm
MS Or. 2627 (v.2), f. 136v

The magnificent decoration on this page – probably the most luxurious and sumptuously illuminated leaf in the entire manuscript – combines Spanish Mudejar (Islamic), Flemish and Portuguese motifs. The border shielding the text boasts intricate lacy arabesques and a unique lozenge-shaped word panel. On its deep blue background, written in gold letters, are the opening words of Isaiah – *Hazon Yesha'yahu* (Isaiah's Vision). The outer border comprises lavish gold scrolls on a green ground with red and blue inlays.

This particular type of embellished opening, with juxtaposed borders, can be found only in Volume Two of the Lisbon Bible. Other features of these openings are initial word panels with black filigree, and a lack of massoretic annotations. In this example a deep red border, covered in thin gold paisley style pattern and stylized flowers, appears alongside a luxurious flowery border garnished with golden dots and living creatures. The prototypes for the creatures and other elements incorporated in the lush frames of the Lisbon Bible probably originated in a 15th-century Latin Breviary from Castile.

48 Opening to Amos
The Lisbon Bible
Hebrew Bible in three volumes
Lisbon, Portugal
1482
295 x 245 mm
MS Or. 2627 (v.2), f. 252r

49 Opening to Chronicles
The Lisbon Bible
Hebrew Bible in three volumes
Lisbon, Portugal
1482
300 x 240 mm
MS Or. 2628 (v.3), f. 1v

This embellished leaf with burnished gold fillets looks astonishingly flawless five centuries after it was first painted, a testament to the high standard of the technique that was used in preparing the Lisbon Bible. It is generally acknowledged that the Bible was illuminated by a team of skilled artists and craftsmen in a Lisbon workshop, which was active from about 1469 to 1496 producing elegant manuscripts about 30 of which have survived.

This carpet page owes its arresting appeal to the superb micrographic design occupying its centre, and the gorgeous lacy surface surrounding it. The text penned in minute script, in the six-petalled rosette and surrounding semicircles, is the end of a poem written in the form of a good-humoured contest in which the Bible and the Talmud are each claiming superiority over the other. It was composed by Yosef ben Yehudah Zark, a 15th-century Catalonian poet.

50 A poem by Yosef ben Yehudah Zark
The Lisbon Bible
Hebrew Bible in three volumes
Lisbon, Portugal
1482
300 x 240 mm
MS Or. 2628 (v.3), f. 185r

51 Opening to Leviticus
The Almanzi Pentateuch
Lisbon, Portugal
1480–90
170 x 117 mm
MS Add. 27167, f. 148v

The dainty arabesques in the initial word panel of this Pentateuch, and the bird and floral motifs in its outer border are reminiscent of the Lisbon Bible (*figs*. 43–50). Other similarities in their decoration programme leave little doubt that both manuscripts were created in the same Lisbon workshop, which was seemingly active from 1469 to 1496. The manuscript is named after its last owner Joseph Almanzi, (1801–60) a renowned bibliophile whose Hebrew manuscript collection was acquired by the British Museum in 1865 and is now in the British Library.

Openings to Lamentations, which is read during the Fast of Av (*Tisha'h be Av*), a fast commemorating the destruction of the Jerusalem Temple (70 AD), were usually left plain in Hebrew manuscripts. This exquisite opening page, with stunning paisley-style lacework and rich flourishes extending to the margins, is therefore quite exceptional. The only sombre element is the black ink used in its execution.

52 Opening to Lamentations
The Almanzi Pentateuch
Lisbon, Portugal
1480–90
170 x 117 mm
MS Add. 27167, f. 419v

53 Opening of Leviticus
The Duke of Sussex's Portuguese Pentateuch
Lisbon, Portugal
1480–90
196 x 138 mm
MS Add. 15283, f. 88r

The illuminations in this manuscript stylistically resemble those in the Almanzi Pentateuch and the Lisbon Bible (*figs.* 43–52), strongly suggesting that they were decorated in the same workshop. What differs here is the Hebrew handwriting used for copying the main body of the text. The square calligraphy of the Lisbon Bible has here been replaced by an elegant semi-cursive African Sephardi hand, but the headings and marginal notes are in Hebrew square script. The latter type of script was more common in Bibles, as seen in many earlier examples (*figs.* 5, 19, 33–4). However, in Biblical codices made in Italy scribes often utilized semi-cursive rabbinic writing.

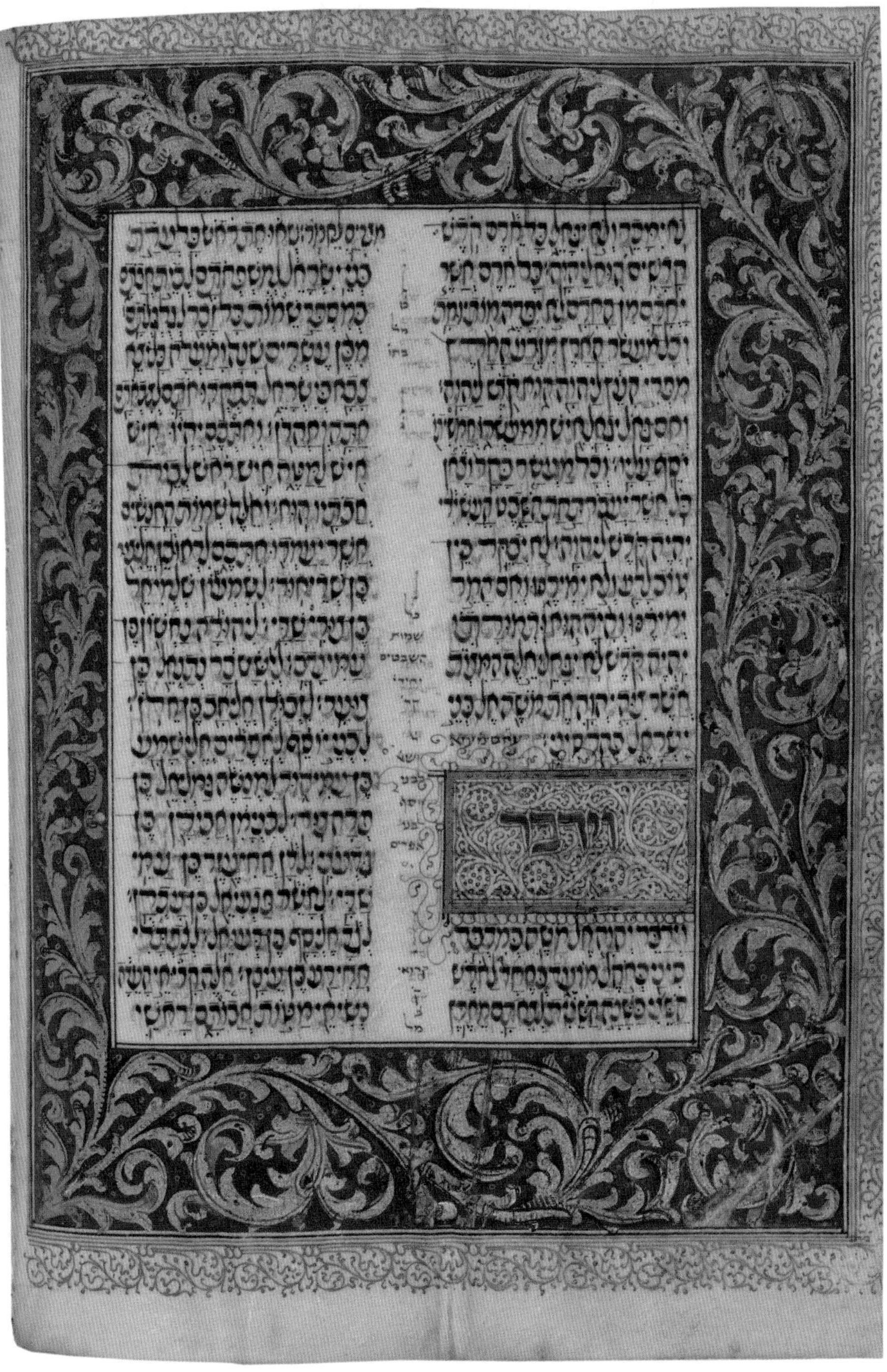

None of the 30 surviving manuscripts created in the aforementioned Lisbon workshop (*figs.* 43–52) contains realistic human forms or textual illustrations. Embellished frames consisting of floriated designs, exquisite ink-drawn filigree and ornamental gold lettering, are the characteristic components of works produced in this thriving atelier. This opening provides yet another splendid example of its artisans' refined craftsmanship and masterly skills.

54 Opening to Numbers
The Duke of Sussex's Portuguese Pentateuch
Lisbon, Portugal
1480–90
196 x 138 mm
MS Add. 15283, f. 114v

55–56 Opening to Leviticus
Pentateuch with Rashi's commentary
Germany
first half of the 14th century
215 x 155 mm
MS Or. 2696, ff. 194v-195r

The leaf above shows the beginning of Leviticus, while the page opposite displays the final section of Exodus, with its lines set out in the shape of a goblet. Here and elsewhere in the manuscript the biblical text is written in a vocalized Ashkenazi square script (Hebrew writing characteristic of Franco-German lands). Penned close to the sacred text are the massoretic notes. Rashi's commentary appears in the outer margins in columns of minute semi-cursive script. Rashi, an acronym of Rabbi Solomon ben Itshaki (1040–1105), was the greatest medieval commentator of the Hebrew Bible. His commentary was often incorporated in biblical manuscripts and later in

printed Bibles. The word *Va-Yikra*, from the verse, 'And the Lord called unto Moses' (Leviticus 1:1), inscribed in letters of gold in the ornate panel opposite, appears also as a catchword at the foot of the page above (which would be read first in Hebrew). Catchwords were medieval scribal devices intended to ensure the correct order of sheets and leaves in a manuscript. Decorated with paisley-style designs in red and black penwork, the panel border features eight medallions filled with animals and grotesques. Its upper corners sprout into foliage sprigs enhanced in gold and silver.

57 Opening to Numbers
Pentateuch with Rashi's commentary
Germany
first half of 14th century
215 x 155 mm
MS Or. 2696, f. 257v

The word in the window-shaped panel reads *Va-Yedaber* from the verse, 'And the Lord spoke' (Numbers 1:1). Its gilded letters lie on a surface divided into 11 red and blue compartments displaying medallions inhabited by fabulous animals and grotesques. Stylized flowers emerge from the upper corners of the panel. The Ashkenzi script and German style of illuminations point to Germany as the manuscript's place of origin; however, the name of the punctuator and masoretic scribe – Mordecai ben Hayim Amandante – suggests an Italian connection. The link with Italy is further attested by the sale notes of several Italian owners.

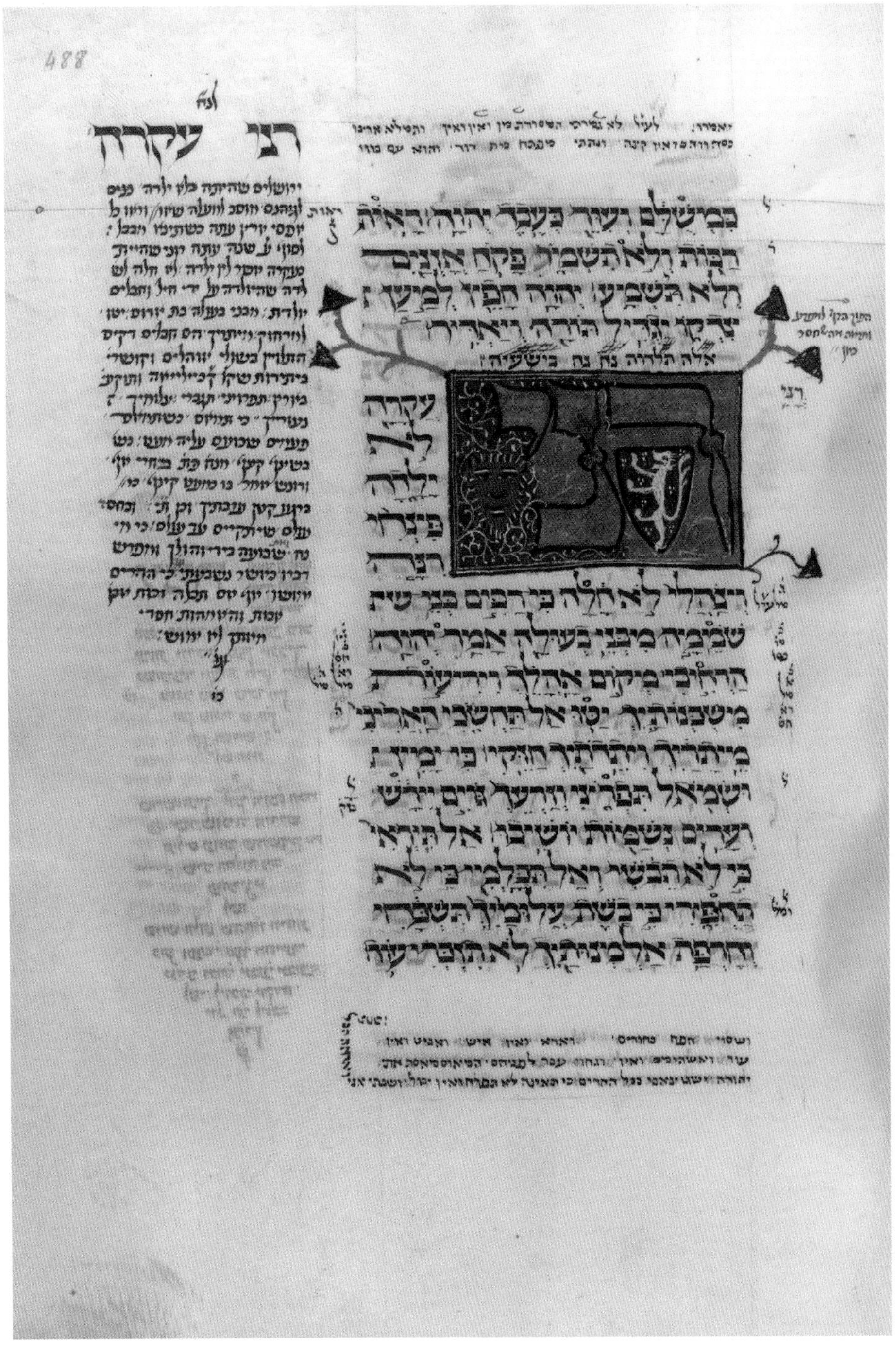

The gilded word *Roni* penned in the panel translates as 'sing' from the opening verse: 'Sing, O barren, thou that didst not bear...' (Isaiah 54:1). Additional panel decorations include a blue coat of arms showing a white rampant lion, a red grotesque mask and stylized foliage extensions enhanced in gold. The biblical text is bordered by the masoretic glosses, whereas Rashi's interpretations were penned in a narrow column to the left of the main text, which was copied in a neat square Ashkenazi hand.

58 Prophetical readings from *Isaiah*
Pentateuch with Rashi's commentary
Germany
first half of 14th century
215 x 155 mm
MS Or. 2696, f. 488r

59 Opening to Leviticus
Pentateuch with Rashi's commentary and the Aramaic translation
Northern Italy
c. 1460–70
230 x 175 mm
MS Harley 7621, f. 142v

The opening word of Leviticus *Va-Yikra* ('And the Lord called unto Moses') is penned in gold display letters against a lapis lazuli diapered ground. The biblical text is surrounded by a border of bright stylized flowers, filigree ornament background, birds and golden drops. The Aramaic translation is introduced by a smaller word panel of pen and mauve ink tracery topped by an ornamental vase with florid motifs. Samuel the Scribe copied the biblical text and the Onkelos translation in a semi-cursive script, as well as the commentaries in a cursive hand in the outer margins. The elegant ornamentations show a distinct Ferrarese style of illumination.

The gilded initial word and elegant floral embellishments above resemble those shown opposite. What differs here is the vignette portraying Moses addressing the Israelites in illustration to the opening verse of Deuteronomy. This Pentateuch shares many decorative elements with a legal code (*figs.* 103–4), the most conspicuous being the flowers, birds and vases. The existence of a coat of arms elsewhere in the manuscript suggests the patronage of Yoav Emmanuel, whose name appears in the juridical code on the colophon page. The Pentateuch was still in Italy in 1628, as attested by Domenico Caretto's dated censorial note on its last leaf.

60 Opening to Deuteronomy
Pentateuch with Rashi's commentary and the Aramaic translation
Northern Italy
c. 1460–70
230 x 175 mm
MS Harley 7621, f. 254v

61 Rabbi Gamliel and his students
The Forli Sidur
Daily prayer book
Italian rite
Forli, Italy
1383
145 x 110 mm
MS Add. 26968, f. 118r

The opening shown comes from the middle of the Hagadah, the order of service for Passover Eve. The Hagadah is one of the most commonly illustrated texts, even when, as here, it is included in the liturgy for the entire year. The miniature shows a teacher and his students illustrating the words above it: *Rabban Gamliel used to say whoever does not explain these three things on Passover has not fulfilled his obligation, namely, the Paschal lamb, unleavened bread and bitter herb*. The Gothic-style bookcase in which the books, bound with clasps, are stored flat, was customary at the time. This Sidur was copied for Daniel ben Samuel Harofe whose arms appear in the manuscript three times.

An entry in the manuscript names Daniel ben Samuel Harofe as the first owner who might have also been the scribe. Seemingly the family's heraldic shield, this coat of arms also features in the Forli Sidur, which once belonged to Daniel (*fig.* 61). It shows a rampant lion rising from a crested helmet above a shield displaying the family emblem. In imitation of the Christian custom, Italian Jews from the upper echelons devized their own family coats of arms. Jewish usage of armorial bearings, as a trendy status symbol rather than an inherited feudal privilege, was tolerated but not formally recognized, thus primary sources for their identification are lacking.

62 Coat of arms of Daniel Harofe
Daily prayer book
Italian rite
Bertinoro, Italy
1390
140 x 105 mm
MS Or. 2736, f.
(verso of front cover)

63–64 The Exodus from Egypt
Festival prayer book
Italy
1466 and 1427
265 x 195 mm
MS Harley MS 5686, ff. 60v-61r

This double-page miniature shows the Israelites leaving Egypt with Pharaoh's army in pursuit. On the left, leading the crowd, is Moses, with staff in hands, following a pillar of fire (Exodus 13: 21). Splendidly dressed in contemporary garments, the Israelites' faces are clearly discernible. Note the fine features of the youth in the centre of the front row. The fortress on the right-hand page represents *Mitsrayim* (Egypt). On horseback, leading the large armoured corps is the crowned Pharaoh (left), followed by an armoured warrior and finely clad nobleman. The banner inscriptions translate as 'Pharaoh'. The winged, haloed angel in the medallion above represents God's angel who guided the

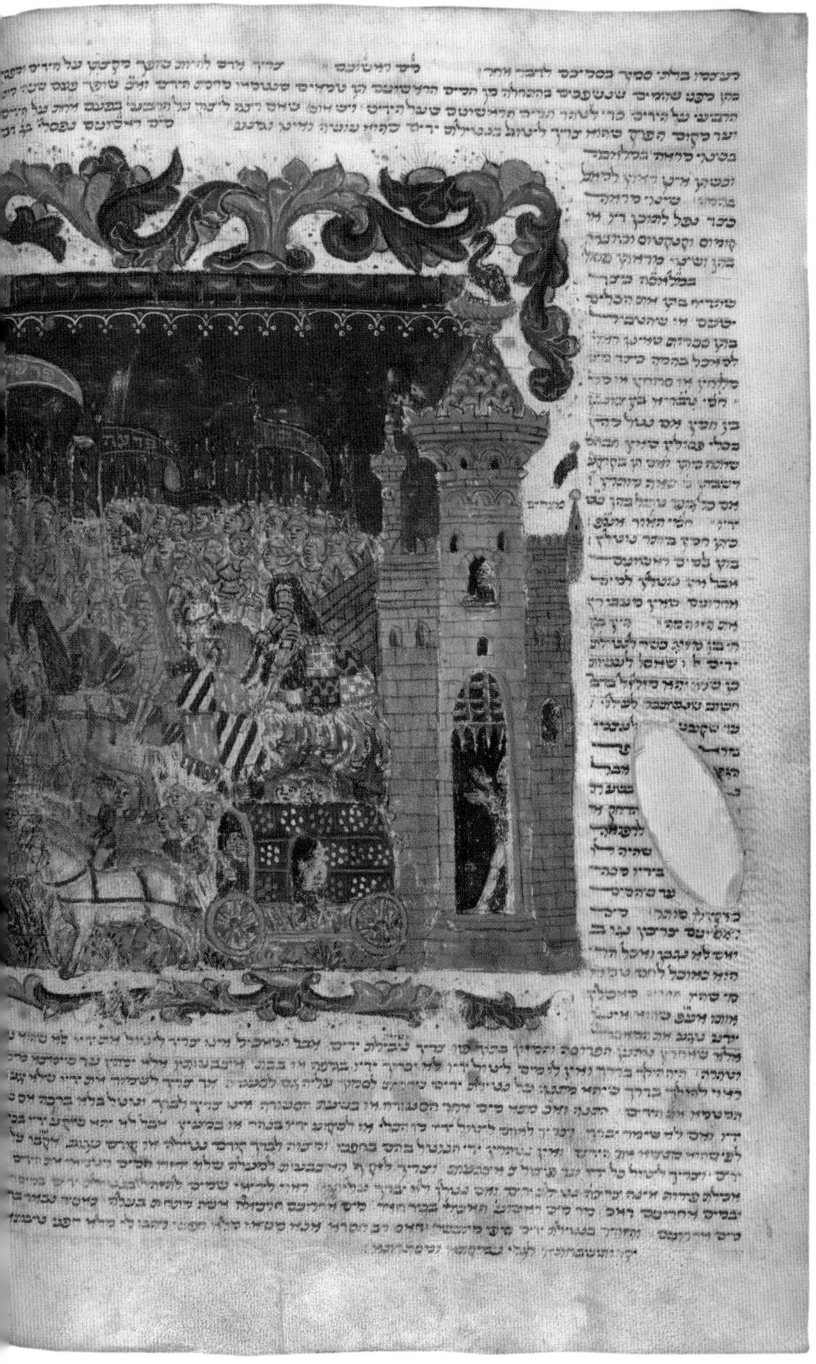

Israelites on their way (Exodus 14:9). Reminiscent of a medieval Italian pageant, this magnificent scene resembles in concept and layout the exodus scenes painted in the Ashkenazi Hagadah (*figs*. 93–4). It comes from the first part of a dual manuscript. The first 384 folios were copied in 1466 by Leon ben Joshua De Rossi of Cesena for Yoav Emmanuel of Reggio, the patron of two other works described here (*figs*. 60, 103–4). The section covering folios 385r-418v, might originally have been a separate manuscript and was copied in 1427 in Bologna by the renowned scribe Isaac ben Obadiah ben David of Forli for Joseph ben Solomon Kohen.

65 Passover eve celebration
Festival prayer book
Italian rite
Italy
1466 and 1427
265 x 195 mm
MS Harley 5686, f. 61v

This charming medieval scene depicts an Italian Passover Eve celebration. Around the table, a group of young men lift a ceremonial two-tier basket filled with green vegetables and other foodstuffs while two men and two women watch from the sides. This and the previous miniature (*figs.* 63–4) provide valuable glimpses into the contemporary dress and ritual customs of northern Italian Jews in the 15th century. In particular, notice the men's pleated *giornea*, a type of sleeveless open-sided garment worn over a tunic (*justaucorps*), and tight leggings, and the women's single-coloured dresses with brocade sleeves in a different shade, thought to be a fashion of Ferrarese origin.

The gilded heading within the finely illuminated panel above reads *Seder 'Inyan Pesah* (The order of Passover). The dog-and-rabbit-chase motif painted within the panel might be an allusion to the mnemonic *YaKNeHaZ* for memorizing the order of benedictions recited when Passover eve occurred at the close of the Sabbath. The letters in this mnemonic stand for *yain* (wine), *kidush* (sanctification), *ner* (light), *havdalah* (separation) and *zeman* (time). Because *YaKNeHaZ* sounds like the German expression *jag den Has* (hunt the hare), some medieval Hagadah manuscripts include pictures of dogs chasing rabbits, or elaborate hunting scenes.

66 Opening of the Passover liturgy
Festival prayer book
Italian rite
Italy
c. 15th century
300 x 240 mm
MS Add. 19064, f. 37v

67 *Ethics of the Fathers*
Festival prayer book in two volumes
Italian rite
Florence, Italy
1441
340 x 245 mm
MS Add. 19944 (v.1), f. 112r

This is the opening to the *Ethics of the Fathers*, a mishnaic treatise comprising the moral teachings of some 60 Jewish sages who lived from 300 BC to 200 AD. Complementing it is Maimonides' commentary translated by Samuel Ibn Tibbon. The fine border with winged *putti* (chubby little boys), bird and floral motifs, is decorated in the humanistic style. Developed initially in Florence in the early 1440's, this style had a tremendous impact on Italy's book production, affecting equally Hebrew manuscript creation. Nowhere is this more evident than in the works of Isaac ben Obadiah ben David of Forli, the scribe of this elegant two-volume prayer book.

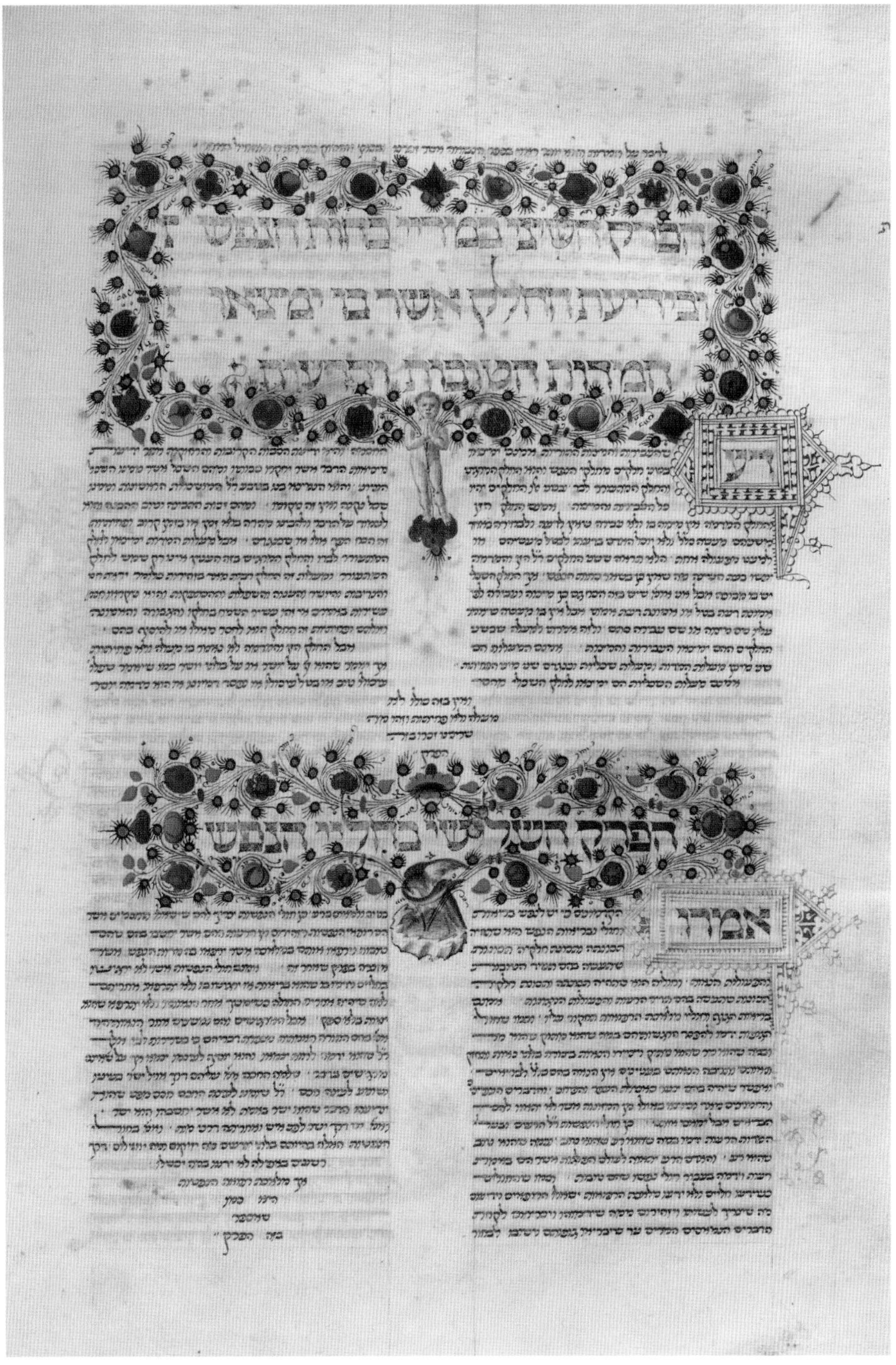

The decorated panels here introduce sections in *Eight Chapters* – Maimonides' foreword to his commentary on the *Ethics of the Fathers*. The scribe Isaac ben Obadiah of Forli used square and semi-cursive scripts for headings and the main body of text respectively. He might also have crafted the exquisite tracery panels in red and blue penwork. Isaac produced some outstanding manuscripts, over 25 of which have survived. His best creations originated in Florence where he worked from 1441 to the end of the 1460's. This is his first Florentine manuscript, which he copied for Salomone di Matassia's sons, Jacob and David, scions of an illustrious banking family from Perugia.

68 Maimonides' *Eight Chapters*
Festival prayer book in two volumes
Italian rite
Florence, Italy
1441
340 x 245 mm
MS Add. 19944 (v.1), f. 113v

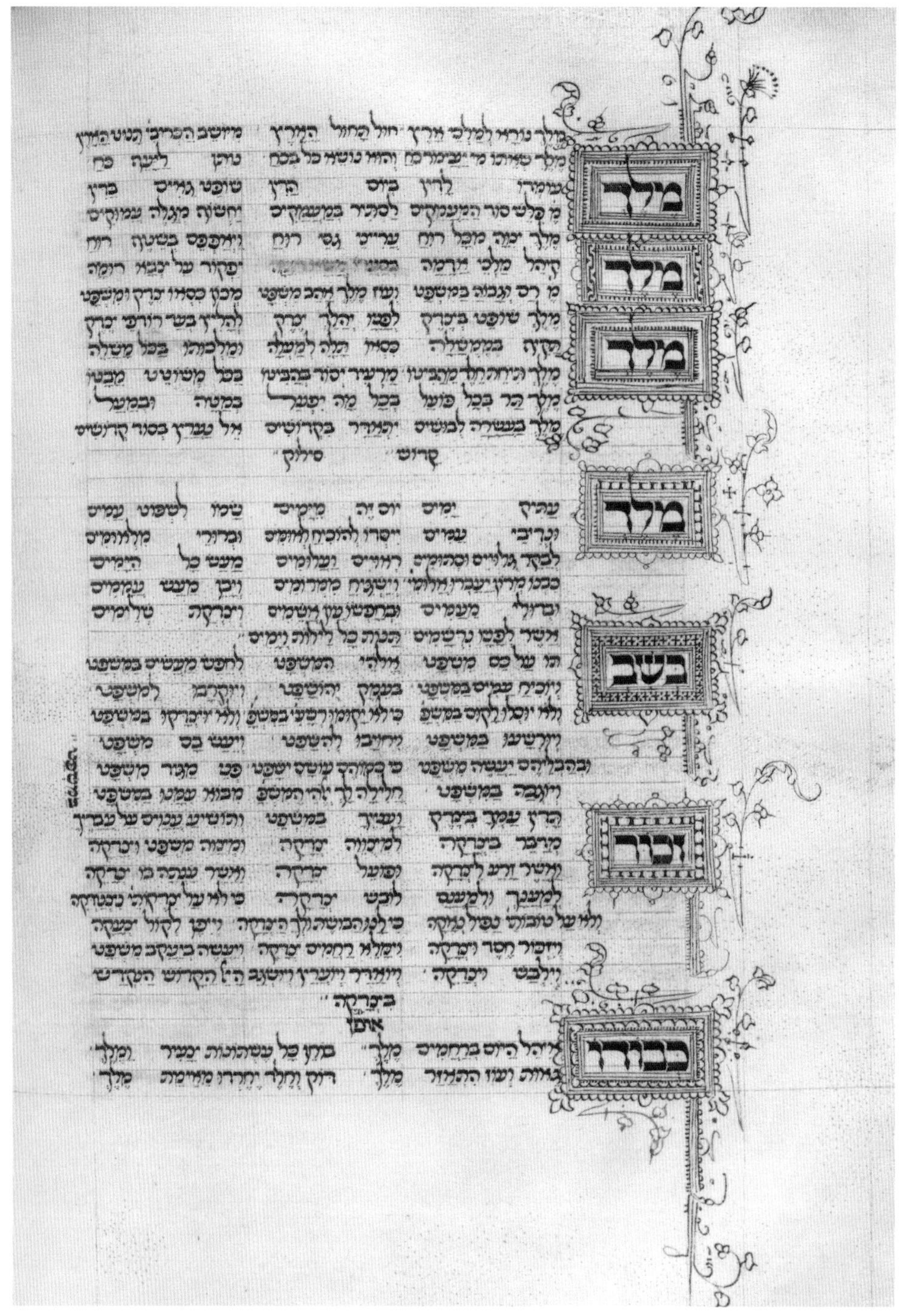

69 Prayer with censor's erasures
Festival prayer book in two volumes
Italian rite
Florence, Italy
1441
340 x 245 mm
MS Add. 19945 (v.2), f. 71v

Exhibited here is part of the liturgy for the first day of the Jewish New Year. Sections extolling the Lord's innumerable attributes are introduced by the Hebrew word *Melekh* (King) written in display characters within dainty red and blue filigree panels. Isaac ben Obadiah, known also as Gaio di Servadio da Forli, penned the text in three columns in his neat semi-cursive Hebrew hand and was probably responsible for creating the filigree word panels also. The erased line of text in the upper section of the middle column attests to expurgatorial interference, undoubtedly by one of three named revisers who inspected the manuscript in 1601, 1613 and 1626 respectively.

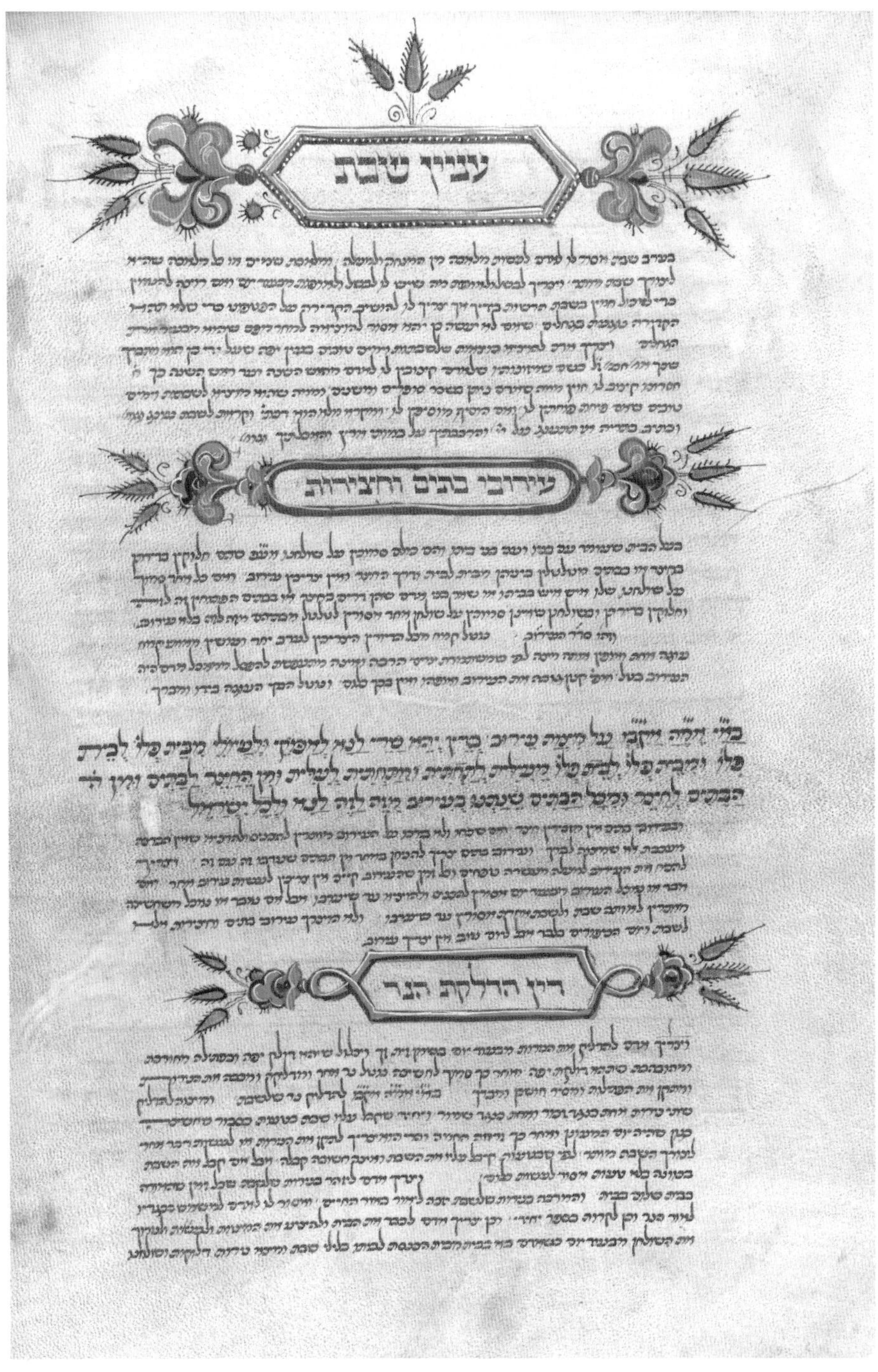
עניין שבת

עירובי בתים וחצירות

דין הדלקת הנר

The opening contains specific Sabbath laws as observed by the Jews of Italy. These include customs for the eve of the festival, rules for setting up an *eruv* (a precinct within which things are allowed to be carried on Sabbath and holidays), and rulings for kindling the Sabbath candles. The unidentified scribe exhibits a particularly fine semi-cursive hand in writing the main text, which is partially vocalized. He used square Hebrew characters for the headings, which are painted in vibrant colours and gold. Exceptionally rich and lavishly illuminated, this Hebrew manuscript rates as one of the finest of the Italian renaissance.

70 Sabbath liturgy
Festival prayer book
Italian rite
Italy
15th century
325 x 225 mm
MS Add. 16577, f. 13v

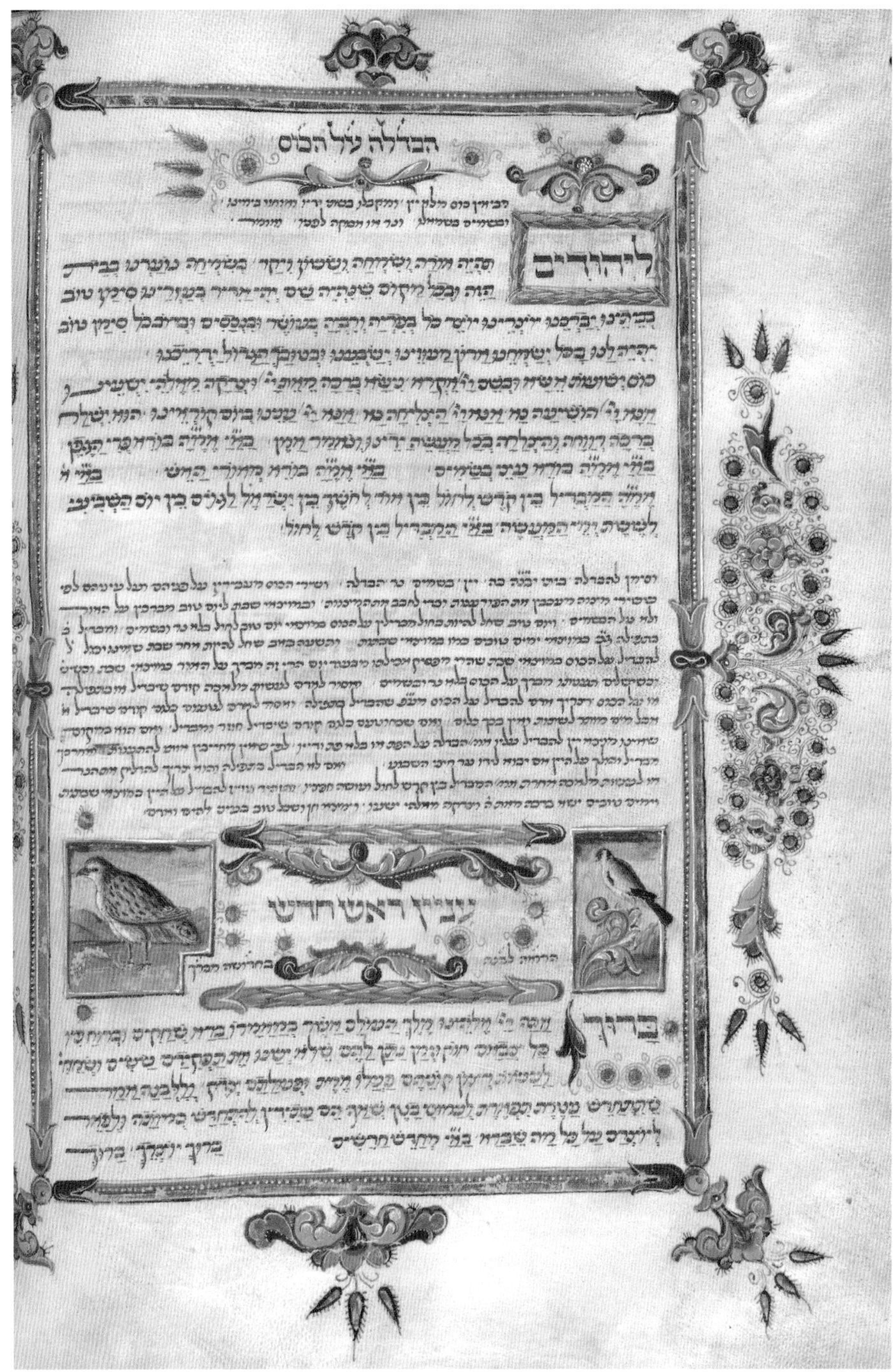

71 Liturgy for the New Moon
Festival prayer book
Italian rite
Italy
15th century
325 x 225 mm
MS Add. 16577, f. 27v

This magnificent opening contains the blessing over wine and laws relating to the *Havdalah* ceremony (separation), followed by the blessing for the New Moon. The text is enclosed by a brightly coloured border garnished with gold fillets. The heading for the New Moon (*'Inyan Rosh Hodesh*) featuring two framed birds, and the marginal floral wreaths speckled with golden dots and leaves are particularly eye-catching. The style of decoration employed throughout the manuscript is Ferrarese, which was common to the area of the Adriatic coast south of Ferrara. However, through lack of a colophon the artists' identity remains unknown.

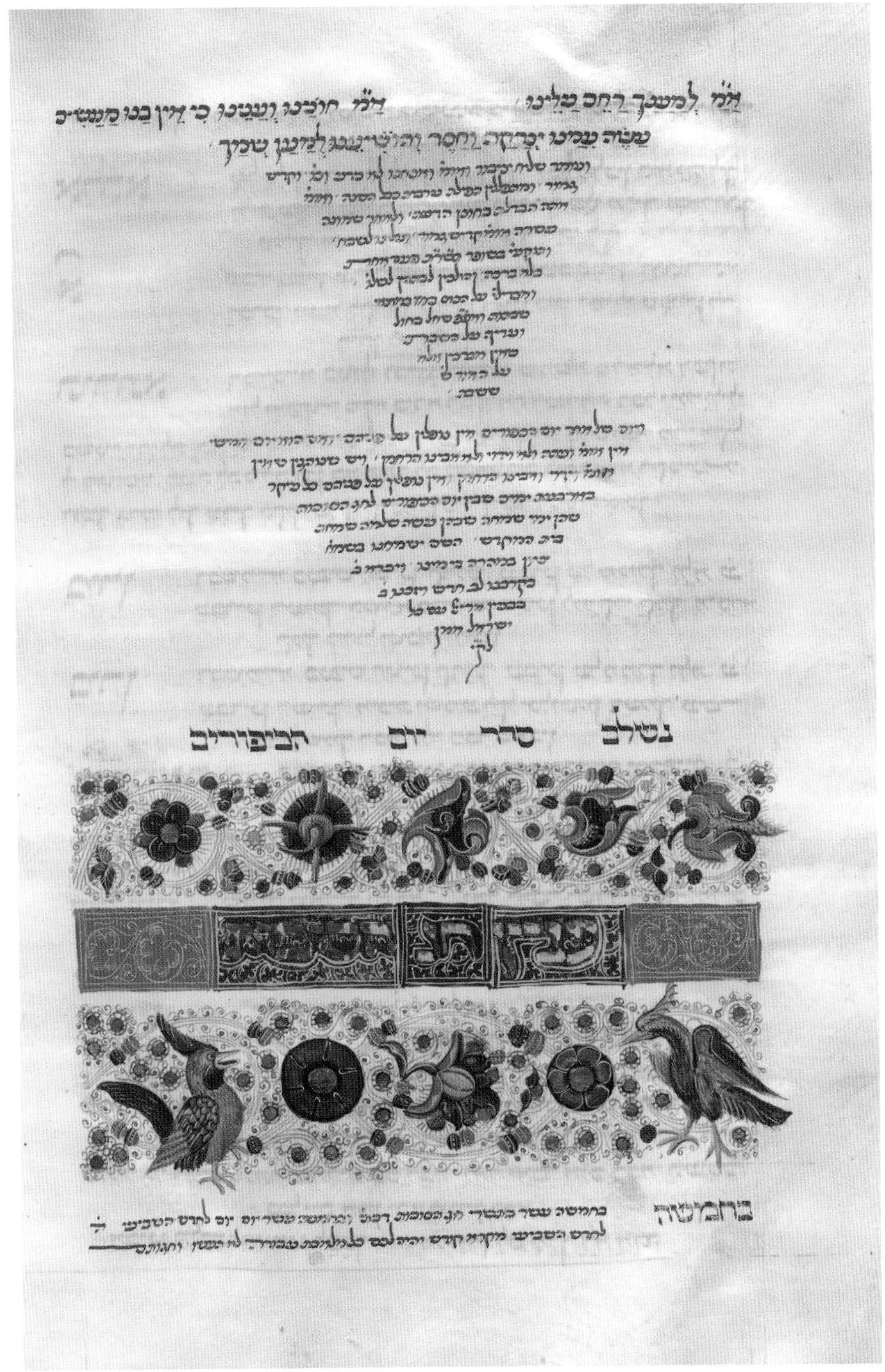

The exhibited page contains the final section of the service for the Day of Atonement (*Yom Kipur*) and the beginning of the service for the Feast of Tabernacles (*Sukot*). The latter is introduced by a splendid heading embellished with flowers and exotic birds rendered in strong, brilliant colours and gold. The first owner of this prayer book was Abraham ben Jacob whose name appears on the profusely illuminated last page. Other names signed in the manuscript are those of three Christian censors who in turn inspected it in 1575, 1611 and 1688, but left no marks of expurgation.

72 Liturgy for the Feast of Tabernacles
Festival prayer book
Italian rite
Italy
15th century
325 x 225 mm
MS Add. 16577, f. 260v

73 Poem for the second day of Passover
Festival prayers, rite of Avignon
Provence, France
1541
225 x 165 mm
MS Or. 10733, f. 90r

The custom of Avignon belonged to the Provencal rite which the Jewish communities of Avignon, Carpentras, Cavaillon and L'Isle sur la Sorgue (known collectively as the Comtat Venaissin) followed continually from the Middle Ages through to the 19th century. Displayed here is the beginning of a liturgical hymn for the second day of Passover. The main text was copied in a neat semi-cursive Provencal style of Hebrew writing. The brightly coloured border with lush vegetation, birds and a *putto* fighting a fabulous beast recalls embellished frames in Hebrew manuscripts created in Italy and Portugal a century earlier. However, the artistry here is cruder and not as skilled.

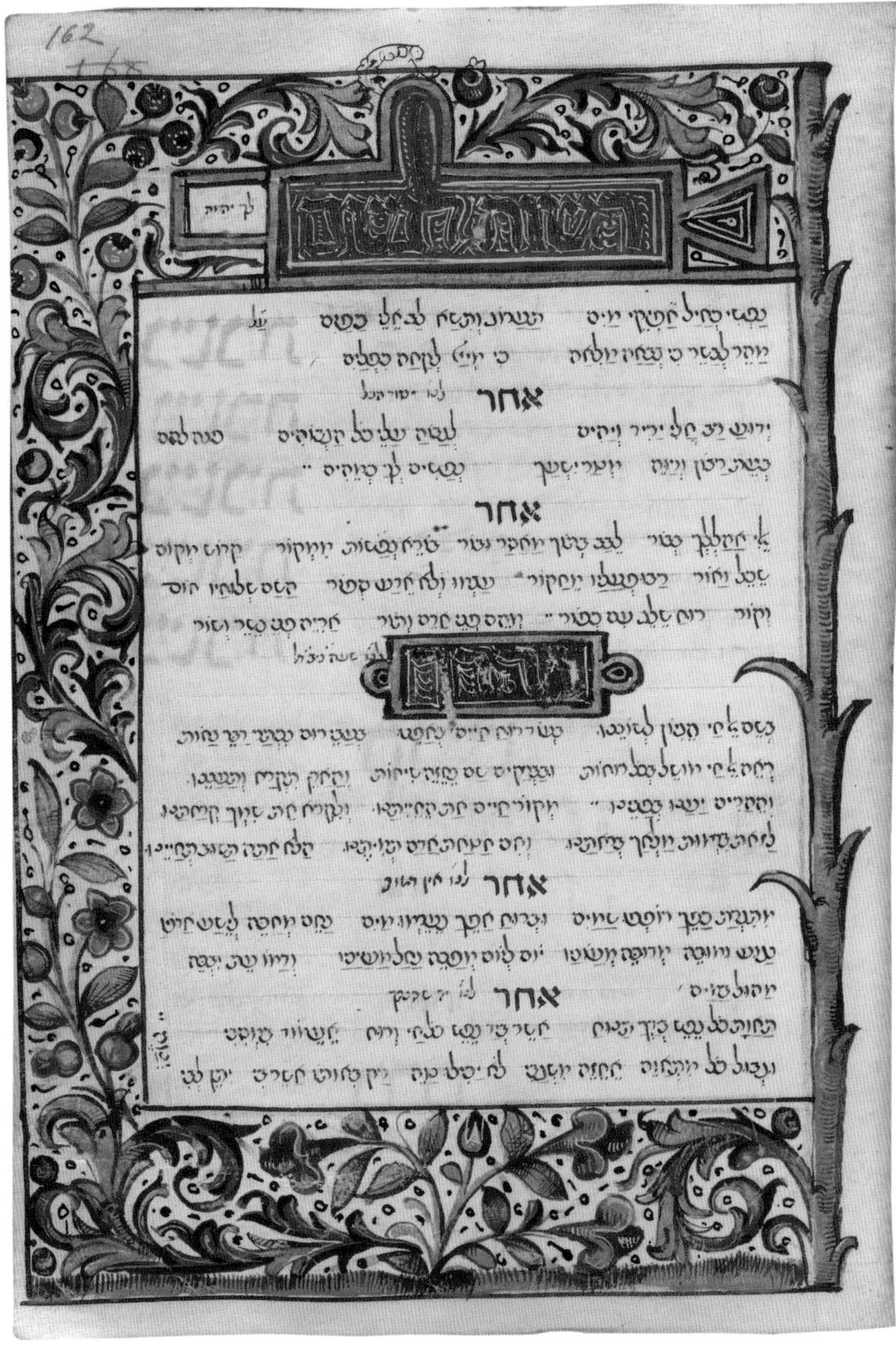

As a result of prolonged isolation from fellow Jews in other lands, Provencal Jews from the Comtat Venaissin developed their own folklore, architecture, calligraphy and, naturally, their individual liturgy. They continued to copy their liturgical texts by hand centuries after printing began, hence the fair number of surviving manuscripts. Seen here is the beginning of a *Reshut lageshem* (prayer for rain), which is recited on the eighth day of *Sukot*, or Feast of Tabernacles. The colourful border decoration of fleshy scrolls and leaves is augmented by red and blue berries, most probably a native element.

74 Prayer for rain
Festival prayers, rite of Avignon
Provence, France
1541
225 x 165 mm
MS Or. 10733, f. 162r

75 Revelation at Mount Sinai
Festival prayers for *Shavu'ot* (Weeks or Pentecost) and *Sukot*(Tabernacles)
German rite
Southern Germany
c. 14th century
315 x 225 mm
MS Add. 22413, f. 3r

The gilded word *Adon* (the Lord) in the panel above opens the liturgical poem 'The Lord has taken care of me', which is recited during *Shavu'ot*, a feast celebrating the giving of the Torah to the Israelites. The miniature depicts Moses receiving the Tablets of the Law on Mount Sinai with Aaron and the Israelites standing in prayer. Trumpets and rams' horns pierce through clouds, marking the occasion. The men were painted with ordinary features while the women have animal heads. The latter was a device used in 14th-century Hebrew illuminated manuscripts from southern Germany, probably in an effort to evade the ban on painting human forms, especially of women.

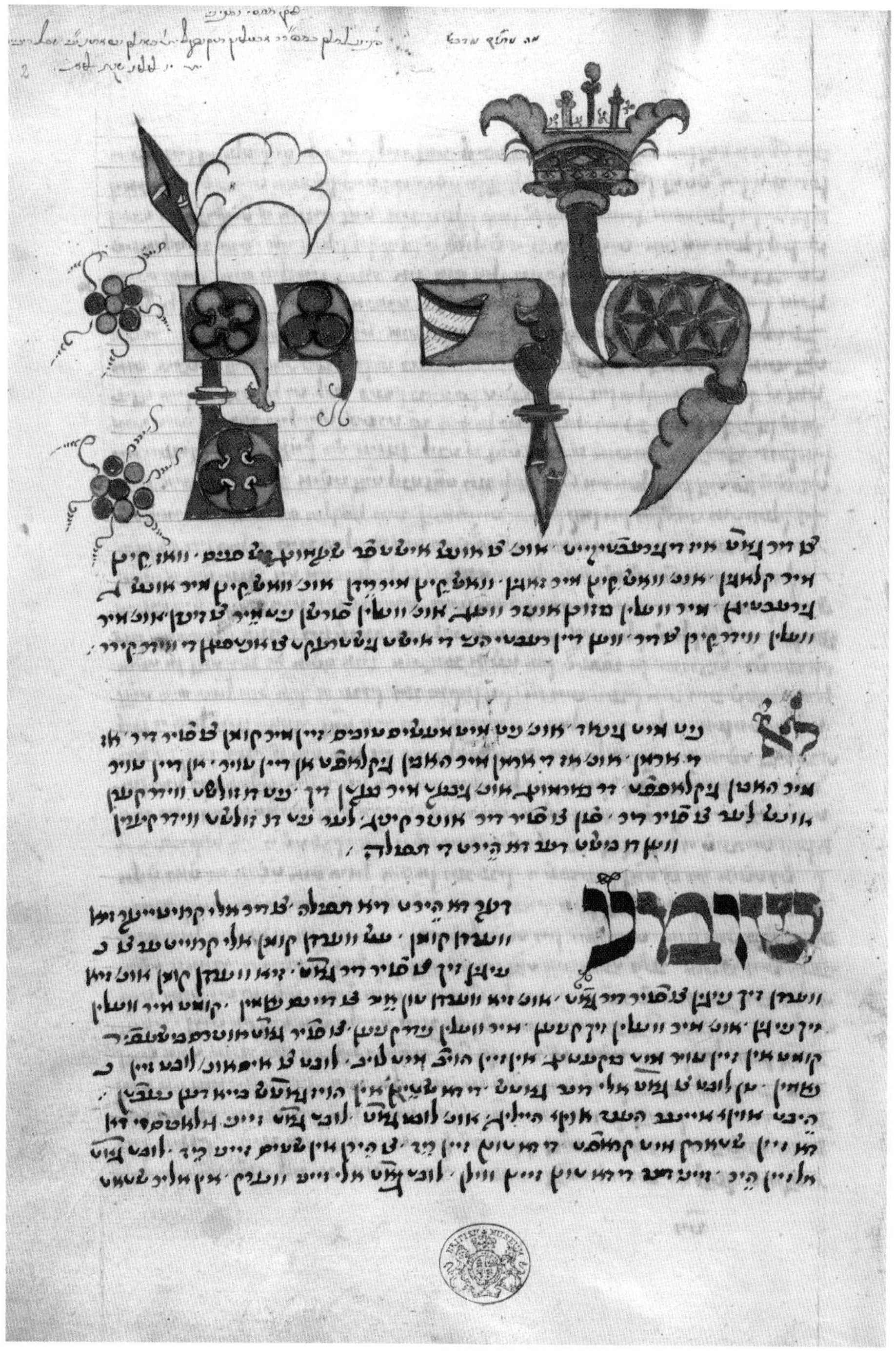

Regarded as the most beautiful Yiddish handwritten book in the British Library's collection, this manuscript boasts many decorations and exquisite ornamental letters. The opening words seen here, *Lekha Adonai* ('To you my Lord'), are written in display characters embellished with floral and abstract designs. The first letter sprouts into a kingly crown, whereas the last forms into a rippled feather. The copyist of this manuscript, Isaac bar Mordecai ha-Kohen, called Isaac Lankosh of Cracow, is likely also to have been responsible for the artistic input.

76 Opening of the penitential liturgy
Festival prayer book
German rite
c. 1560
355 x 255 mm
MS Add. MS 27071, f. 2r

77 Unleavened bread
The Hispano-Moresque Hagadah
Service book for Passover eve
Castile, Spain
c. 1300
160 x 120 mm
MS Or 2737, f. 22r

The Hagadah, which denotes 'telling' or 'narration', is the Hebrew service book used in Jewish homes on Passover Eve to celebrate the Israelites' miraculous deliverance from Egyptian bondage. The central roundel is a stylized illustration of the *Matsah*, which represents the unleavened bread that the Israelites took with them when hurrying out of Egypt. It is one of the obligatory foods consumed at the *Seder* (order) – the Passover Eve celebration. As in other medieval Spanish Hagadah manuscripts, the *Matsah* occupies nearly all the space on the page. Its intertwined structure, which vaguely evokes an astrolabe, and the central rosette draw on Moorish abstract designs.

Apart from the *Matsah* (unleavened bread), one other essential foodstuff consumed on Passover eve is the *Maror* (bitter herb), which symbolizes the bitter life endured by the Hebrew slaves while in Egyptian bondage. In this miniature the bitter herb is represented by a large cluster of green leaves, beneath a decorated arch. The Hebrew word in the Gothic panel topping the herb spells *Maror*. This stylized depiction of the bitter herb is characteristic of medieval Spanish Hagadot. The unleavened bread and the bitter herb are regarded as the oldest illustrations to the Hagadah text.

78 Bitter herb
The Hispano-Moresque Hagadah
Service book for Passover eve
Castile, Spain
c. 1300
160 x 120 mm
MS Or. 2737, f. 22v

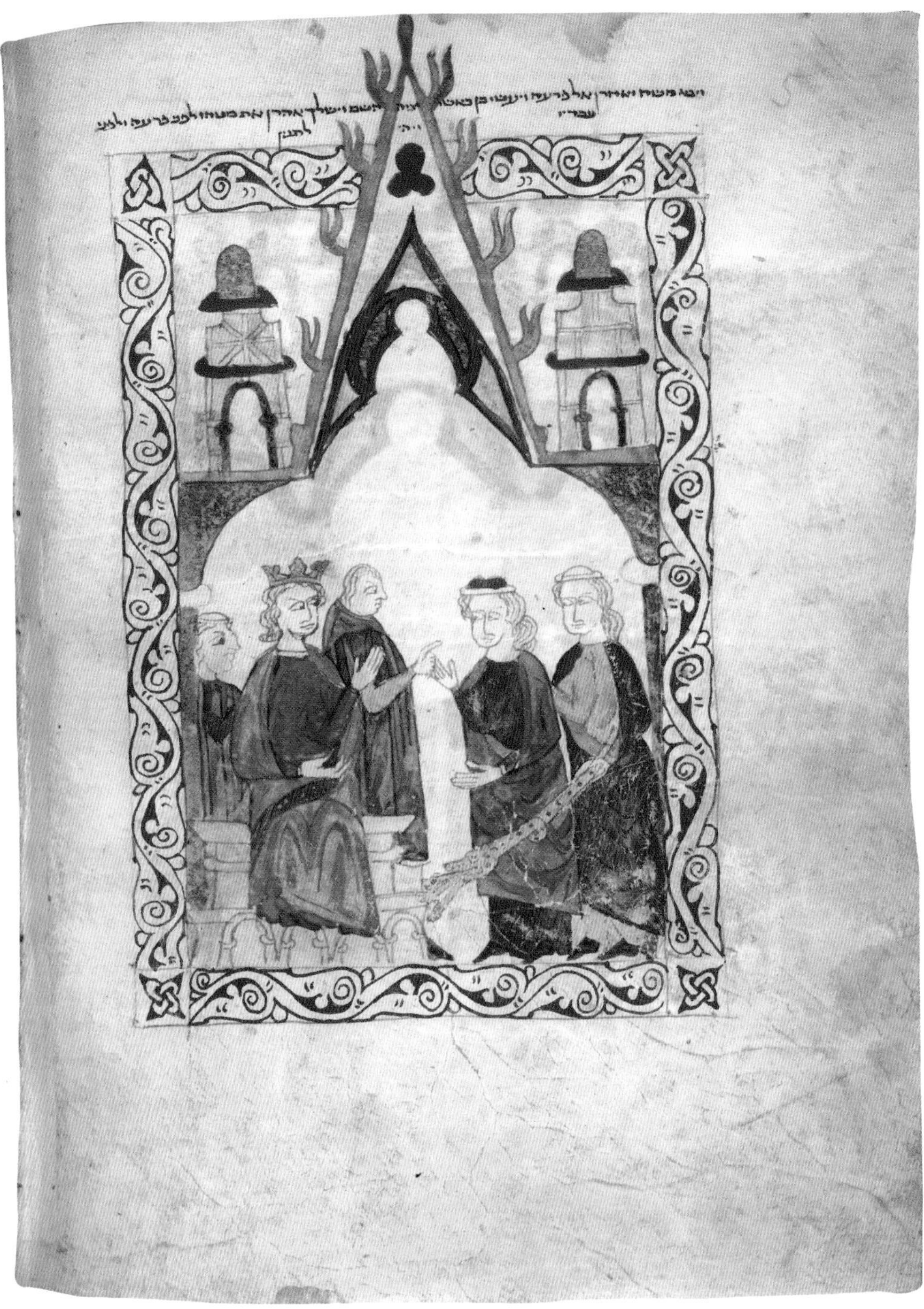

79 Moses and Aaron at Pharaoh's court
The Hispano-Moresque Hagadah
Service book for Passover eve
Castile, Spain
c. 1300
160 x 120 mm
MS Or. 2737, f. 63v

This Passover Hagadah contains 66 full-page illuminations, which feature episodes from Exodus, a scene of the binding of Isaac and several others depicting Passover preparations. Probably two artists worked on the miniatures, which have been painted in bright and pastel colour washes in a rather primitive style. However, the lack of a colophon, a characteristic shared by Hagadah manuscripts produced in medieval Spain, prevents their identification. The scene shows Pharaoh and his attendants watching Moses and his brother, Aaron, whose rod turned into a snake and swallowed the magicians' rods (Exodus 7:10).

Since the *Matsah* (unleavened bread) is essential to the observance of the Passover holiday, its proper and careful preparation is a centuries-old Jewish tradition. This pictorial rendition of a Jewish bakery in medieval Spain prior to the Passover festival provides an insight into the life and customs of Spanish Jews at the turn of the 14th century. It shows the baker pushing the roundels of unleavened bread into a large open oven with the aid of a shovel. Two women carrying trays of raw *Matsah* wafers wait to have them baked. The linear pattern marked on the round cakes prevented the dough from rising during the baking process.

80 Baking the *matzah*
The Hispano-Moresque Hagadah
Service book for Passover eve
Castile, Spain
c. 1300
160 x 120 mm
MS Or. 2737, f. 88r

81 Scenes from Exodus
The Golden Hagadah
Service book for Passover eve
Catalonia
c. 1320
247 x 198 mm
MS Add. 27210, f. 10v

The Golden Hagadah has been described as the most sumptuously adorned and best preserved of all surviving illuminated 14th-century Spanish Hagadot. The manuscript owes its fame to the preliminary 14 full-page miniatures executed on diapered gold leaf surfaces. Created by two artists in the contemporary French Gothic style, the miniatures illustrate 71 scenes based on Genesis, Exodus and the Midrash (commentaries on the Torah). The upper scenes show Moses before the burning bush (right), and Moses and his family returning to Egypt (left). Beneath, Moses and Aaron perform miracles before the elders of Israel (lower right), and appear at Pharaoh's court (lower left).

The elaborate text illustration here represents the *Matsah*, or unleavened bread, one of the essential elements in the Passover ritual. It is adorned with an intricate geometric interlacing strongly reminiscent of Islamic design. In medieval Hagadot, the unleavened bread is usually represented as a circular decorated wafer. In Italian and German Hagadot, the *Matsah* wafer is occasionally pictured being held or lifted up by men. In Spanish Hagadot, illustrations of the unleavened bread tend to be fairly large and often fill a whole page, as this example shows.

82 The unleavened bread
The Golden Hagadah
Service book for Passover eve
Catalonia
c. 1320
247 x 198 mm
MS Add. 27210, f. 44v

83 The *Halel* praise
The Golden Hagadah
Service book for Passover eve
Catalonia
c. 1320
MS Add. 27210, f. 55r

Hebrew script plays an important role in manuscript ornamentation as clearly illustrated in this opening, which contains a section from the *Halel*. The *Halel* or Praise is the name given in the Jewish liturgy to Psalms 113–18, which are recited on Passover eve and other festive occasions. Several characters in the illuminated keyword *Yehalelukha* (You will be praised) form the basis of the leaf decoration. The scribe used the exaggerated ascending serifs of two adjacent *lamed* letters to frame the upper palmette strip decorated with lateral vine tendrils. Likewise, by elongating the descending stroke of the letter *khaf*, he created an attractive text divider with asymmetric ivy extensions.

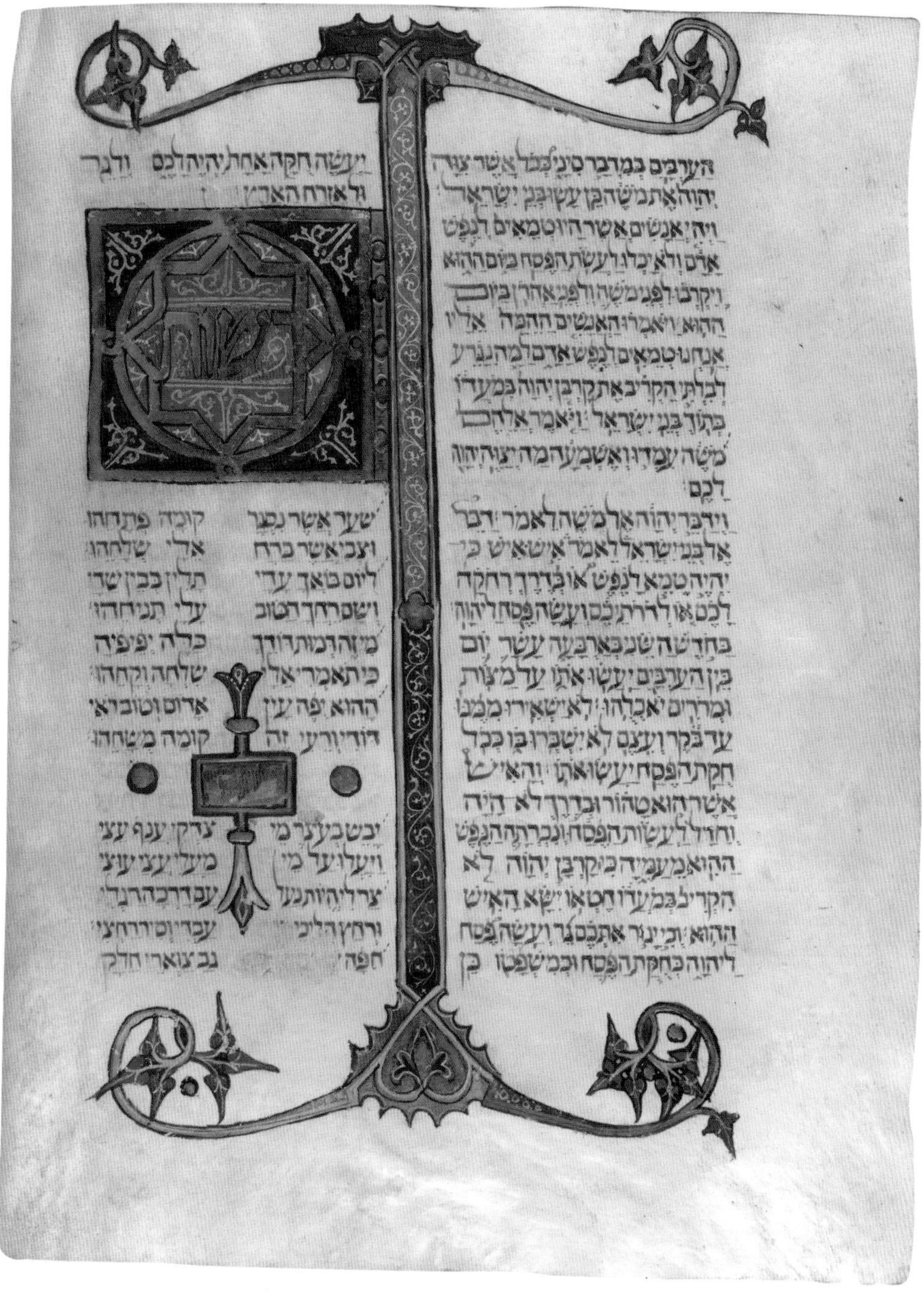

This embellished leaf comprises readings and a special liturgical poem (*reshut*) for the end of Passover. The main ornamentation consists of an inner decorated band with curled ivy extensions, and a gold-framed square title panel. The cusp in the lower section of the band, enclosing a palmette motif, is traceable in Muslim art. Liturgical poems (*piyyutim*) accompanied the mandatory prayers and were meant to reinforce the experience of worship, particularly during the Jewish holidays. This Hagadah includes some 100 Passover *piyyutim*, some of which were composed by the famed Sephardi poets Solomon Ibn Gabirol (*c.* 1021–58) and Judah Halevi (*c.* 1075–1141).

84 Passover poem
The Golden Hagadah
Service book for Passover eve
Catalonia
c. 1320
Add. 27210, f. 78v

85 Passover ritual scenes
The Sister Hagadah
Service book for Passover eve
Catalonia
c. 1350
230 x 190 mm
MS Or. 2884, f. 17r

The charming scenes arranged in two compartments illustrate Passover customs: in the upper scene, distribution of *matsah* (unleavened bread) and *haroset* (sweetmeat) by the master of the house; in the lower panels, searching for leaven (right), and house cleaning before the festival (left). This manuscript shows many iconographic similarities to the more famous Golden Hagadah, hence its namesake – the Sister Hagadah. The biblical cycles in both manuscripts were probably inspired by a common model, but the iconography here is cruder.

In the Sister Hagadah shown here, there are 34 full-page panels illustrating 86 episodes from Genesis and Exodus, and five ritual scenes. This full-page miniature portrays a medieval Jewish family celebrating Passover. The master of the house and members of his household are gathered round a festive table on which are placed Passover utensils and two open Hagadot. Under the table there are two cats. The imagery displays Franco-Gothic and Italian elements, the latter reflected particularly in the architectural and sartorial details, such as turban-like headgear and caps.

86 Passover eve ceremony
The Sister Hagadah
Service book for Passover eve
Catalonia
c. 1350
230 x 190 mm
MS Or. 2884, f. 18r

87 The *Halel* praise
The Sister Hagadah
Service book for Passover eve
Catalonia
c. 1350
230 x 190 mm
MS Or. 2884, f. 60v

As already illustrated in an earlier example (*fig.* 83), in Hebrew manuscript ornamentation the script itself fulfils a significant aesthetic role. Here, the power of the exhortations *Yomar* and *Yomeru* ('Let it be declared', Psalm 118: 2–3), which form part of the *Halel* or Praise, is conveyed through enlarged, illuminated words deliberately singled out from the rest of the text and encapsulated in a separate panel.

Portrayed here as old, learned men, each holding an open book, are Yosi the Galilean and Eliezer, two rabbis from the Hagadah narrative. Their names appear in gold in the upper and lower panels. The characters' facial expressions and posture show marked Byzantine and Italian influences. Called the Brother Hagadah because of its striking resemblance to the Rylands Hagadah held in the Rylands Library in Manchester, it is possible that both were created in the same workshop. Recent studies have shown that the Brother Hagadah served in fact as the archetype for its sibling, and that the unidentified artist followed models from an Italian motif book.

88 Rabbi, Yosi the Galilean and Rabbi Eliezer
The Brother Hagadah
Service book for Passover eve
Catalonia
c. 1350–75
273 x 234 mm
MS Or. 1404, f. 14v

89 The hymn *Dayenu*
The Brother Hagadah
Service book for Passover eve
Catalonia
c. 1350–75
273 x 234 mm
MS Or.1404, f. 16r

A common ornamental feature in Spanish Hagadot is the columnar arrangement of keywords from the Passover thanksgiving hymn *Dayenu* ('It would have been enough'), which extols God's generosity towards the Israelites. Penned on two vertical embellished bands the hymnal keywords *Ilu* (had God) and *ve-lo* (without) are repeated, forming a decorative chain. The ligatures of the letters *aleph* and *lamed* in the right-hand chain are particularly attractive, providing a pertinent example of how the letters of the Hebrew alphabet lend themselves to the decorative.

The Barcelona Hagadah lacks the typical prefatory cycle of biblical narratives that normally adorns 14th-century Spanish Hagadot. Instead, all of its pages are filled with images of Passover rituals, biblical and midrashic episodes and symbolic foods. Particularly stunning are the historiated Gothic word panels and lush marginal foliage scrolls, interwoven with humans, birds, hybrids, grotesque and fabulous beasts. Such motifs were common in Latin manuscripts and may have served as prototypes. The man and child depicted in the word panel perform the *Havdalah* ceremony (Separation), which takes place when the close of the Sabbath coincides with the eve of the festival.

90 The *Havdalah* ceremony
The Barcelona Hagadah
Service book for Passover eve
Catalonia
c. 1370
255 x 190 mm
MS Add. 14761, f. 26r

עבדים
היינו
לפרעה במצרים ויוציאנו
ייי אלהינו משם ביד חזקה
ובזרוע נטויה ואלו לא הוציא

91 The Israelites' bondage
The Barcelona Hagadah
Service book for Passover eve
Catalonia
c. 1370
255 x 190 mm
Add. 14761, f. 30v

This magnificent illustration portrays the Israelites' bondage in Egypt. The scene spreading outwards from the panel shows two task masters, one carrying a hammer, the other a whip, overseeing the Hebrew slaves, who include masons, stone carriers, brick makers and a pulley operator. The figures on horseback might represent Pharaoh and an attendant. The gilded word '*Avadim* (slaves) opens a key section in the narrative: 'We were slaves onto Pharaoh in Egypt'. In this Hagadah animals are occasionally depicted performing human activities, a jocular note borrowed from Latin codices. A relevant example is the dog serving wine to a rabbit in the upper section.

Recited at the conclusion of the Passover eve service, the prayer *Le-shanah ha-ba'ah bi-Yerushalayim amen* ('Next year in Jerusalem, amen') expresses the centuries-long Jewish yearning to restore Jerusalem and its Temple. Its eloquent and moving message is captured here in gold ornamental lettering within an embellished panel.

92 Next year in Jerusalem
The Barcelona Hagadah
Service book for Passover eve
Catalonia
c. 1370
255 x 190 mm
MS Add. 14761, f. 88r

93–94 The Exodus from Egypt
The Ashkenazi Hagadah
Service book for Passover eve
Germany or northern Italy
c. 1460
360 x 270 mm
MS Add. 14762, ff. 14v-15r

In this scene illustrating the Flight from Egypt, the Israelites led by Moses (left) flee the Egyptians led by Pharaoh on horseback (right). A 'blue pillar of cloud' separates them, which according to the Midrash guarded the Israelites by halting the Egyptians' arrows. Moses looks up towards the divine hand, an allusion to the 'strong hand and an outstretched arm…', with which God delivered the Israelites. A pillar of fire, represented by a column surmounted by a flaming torch, guides the Israelites on their sea-crossing. The protagonists' facial expressions, as well as their clothes, uniforms and headgear, are clearly conveyed. The style of illumination shows German and Italian influences.

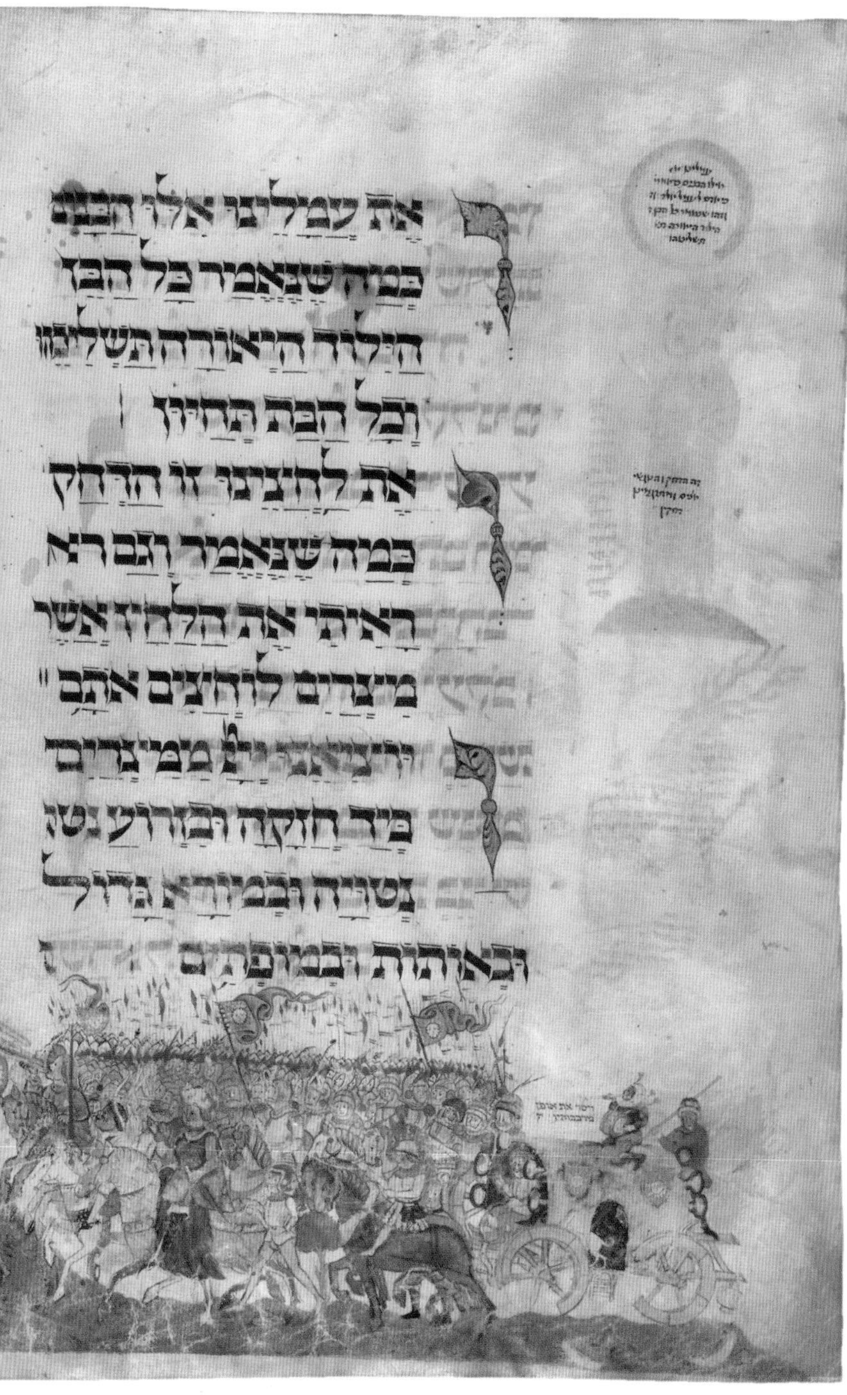

Born in Germany, the famed scribe-artist Joel ben Simeon Feibusch (called Ashkenazi), who participated in the illustration of this Hagadah, paid several lengthy visits to northern Italy, which probably affected his style. Yet he was not the scribe of the manuscript, as thought initially. That significant role was performed by Meir Jaffe, whose masterly calligraphy is simply stunning. A rarity in Hebrew manuscripts, decorated initial Hebrew letters abound in this Hagadah. In the opening shown here, the Hebrew letter *vav* is decorated in five different ways with animal heads, foliage or linefolds. It shows the scribe's attempt to emulate practices employed by Christian copyists.

95 The Rabbis of Bene Brak
The Ashkenazi Hagadah
Service book for Passover eve
Germany or northern Italy
c. 1460
360 x 270 mm
MS Add. 14762, f. 7v

The group of stocky, heavily dressed figures represent the Rabbis of Bene Brak, who feature in the Hagadah narrative. They seem engaged in lively discussion, possibly over the contents of the open book on the carved lectern. Although the colophon names Joel ben Simeon Feibusch as the illuminator, recent studies show that his main task was to represent the patron, Jacob Mattathias in Johannes Bämler's workshop where the manuscript was decorated. Bämler was a known Christian miniaturist and printer from Augsburg. While collaborating with the Christian artists in Bämler's atelier on the Hagadah illuminations, Joel probably ensured that their output suited a Hebrew book.

Probably one of the most elaborate and beautifully crafted initial words in the entire manuscript, *Hodu* (Give thanks) is made of four Hebrew characters whose horizontal serifs are inhabited by a fish, a dog, a lion and a jester. The vertical serifs display undulating, ripple-like folds. The word itself is set within a rectangular green panel featuring a boar-hunting scene with a cityscape in the rear background. It is quite possible that Meir Jaffe, the scribe responsible for copying the text of the Hagadah, also created its exquisite initial word panels.

96 Ornamented Hebrew word
Ashkenazi Hagadah
Service book for Passover eve
Germany or northern Italy
c. 1460
360 x 270 mm
Add. 14762, f. 37v (detail)

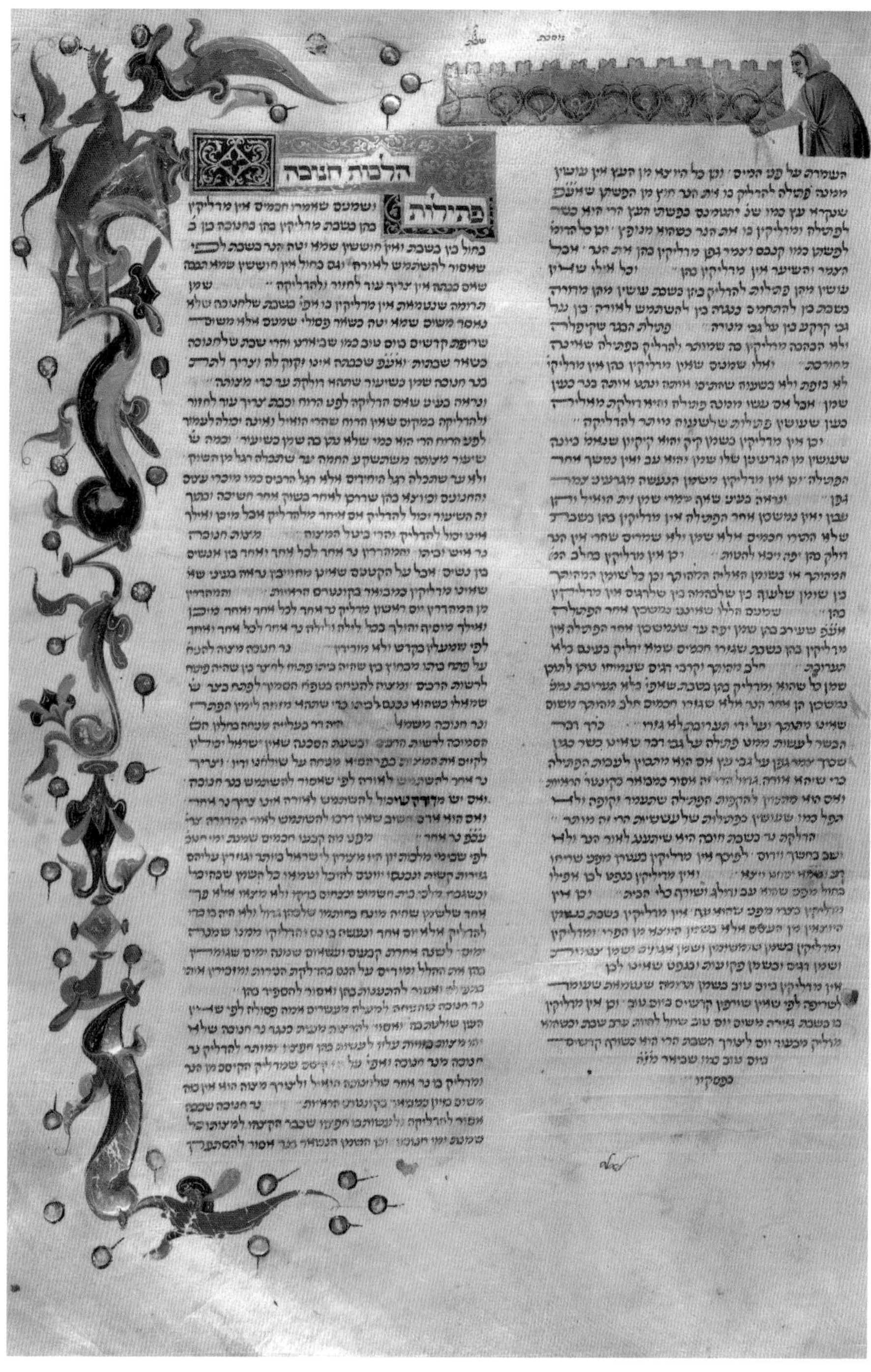

97 Hanukah customs
Legal decisions of Isaiah of Trani the Younger
Perugia, Italy
1374
410 x 280 mm
MS Or. 5024, f. 19r

The illustration in the upper margin depicts the lighting of a Hanukah lamp. This type of wall lamp apparently originated in 13th-century Spain and would have hung outside the entrance to a house during the Hanukah festival. The custom of placing a lamp outdoors, originated in mishnaic times (*c.* 200 AD), following a religious ruling to celebrate the miracle of Hanukah publicly. This handwritten copy of Isaiah di Trani the Younger's decisions (d. 1280) provides a good example of 14th-century Hebrew legal text decoration in Italy. Copied in Perugia, the Bolognese-style illuminations were probably created in the workshop of Nicollo di Giacomo da Bologna (active 1348–99).

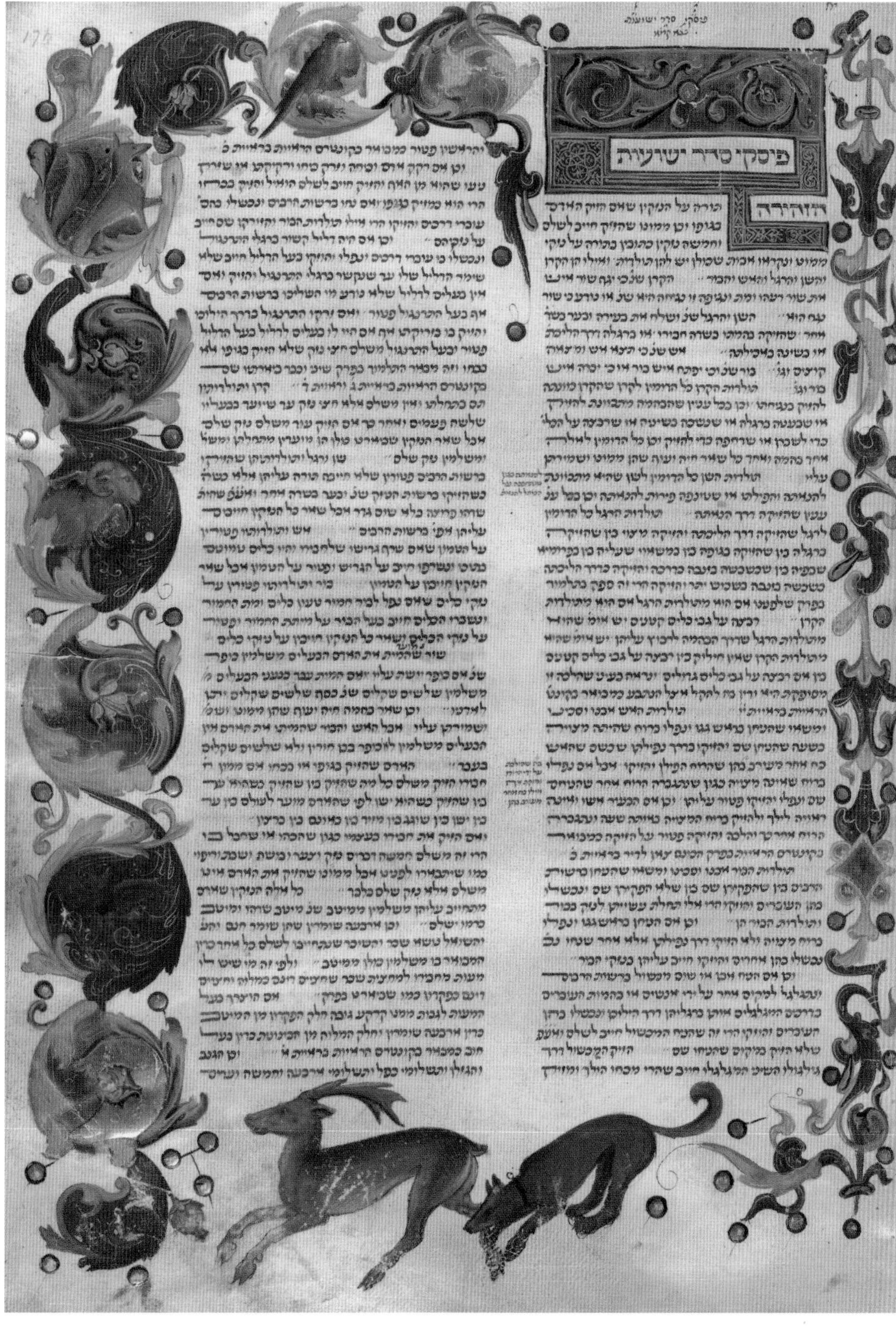

The incipit page of *Seder Nezikin (or Yeshu'ot)*, a key section dealing with damages and rescues, is decorated with a luxuriant border inhabited by faunal motifs, one being a bat. The dog attacking the deer, portrayed in the lower margin, is probably a pictorial interpretation of the intrinsic subject-matter, namely saving victims from persecutors. This copy of Isaiah of Trani's Code was written by Jekuthiel ben Solomon for his teacher Menahem ben Nathan. The ample supplementary matter penned on its end-leaves, such as owners' names, dated deeds of sales and censors' signatures, enable us to recreate in part the manuscript's eventful history.

98 Beginning of *Seder Yeshuot*
Legal decisions of Isaiah di Trani the Younger
Perugia, Italy
1374
410 x 280 mm
MS Or. 5024, f. 171r

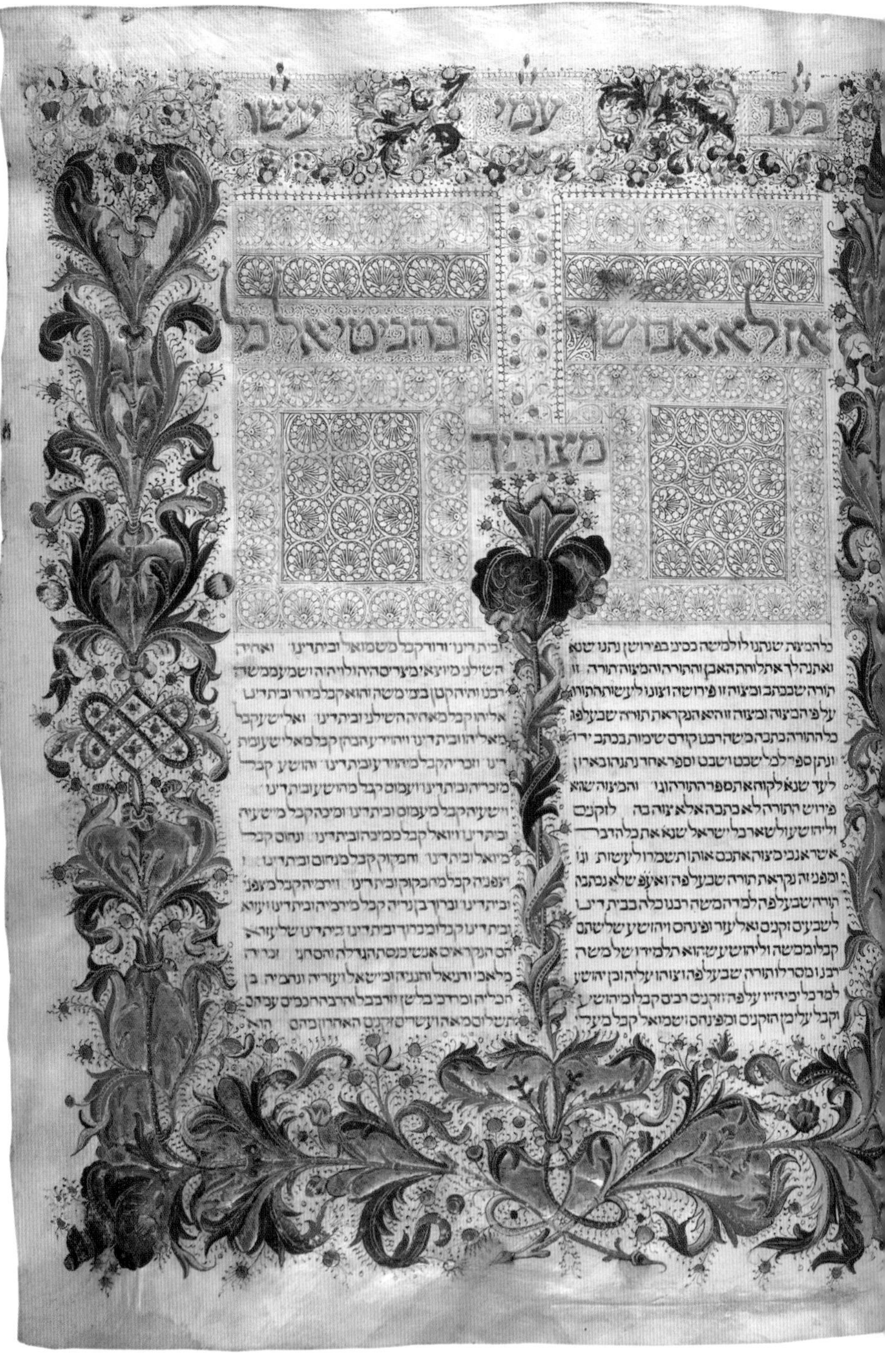

99–100 Introduction to Lisbon Maimonides Legal Code in two volumes
Lisbon, Portugal
1471–72
332 x 240 mm
MS Harley 5698 (v.1), ff. 11v-12r

The *Mishneh Torah* (Repetition of the Law or The Second Law) is the legal Code that Moses Maimonides (*c.* 1138–1204) compiled in Egypt between 1168–78. Probably the greatest contribution to Jewish law ever made by any one individual, the *Mishneh Torah* is virtually the only work Maimonides wrote in Hebrew, Arabic being the language of all his other writings. Each of the Code's 14 books deals with a specific area of human activity and its laws. These sumptuously illuminated leaves derive from a two-volume 15th-century copy of the Code, penned by Solomon ben Alzuk for Don Joseph ben David ben Solomon Ibn Yahya, who was an adviser to the Kings of Portugal.

Although the place of production is not recorded in the manuscript, its Lisbon origin can be construed from its distinctive decorative style. Moreover, the patron, who was born in Lisbon in 1425 and continued to live there until 1495, is known to have commissioned other manuscripts all of which were produced in that city. Its opulent embellishments, ink-drawn filigree surfaces and gold-leaf lettering have earned the manuscript its deserved reputation as a masterpiece of the Portuguese school of Hebrew illumination. The gilded words shown above come from Deuteronomy 4:44: 'And this is the Law which Moses placed before the Children of Israel.'

101 Book of Cleanliness
Lisbon Maimonides
Legal Code in two volumes
Lisbon, Portugal
1471–72
332 x 240 mm
MS Harley MS 5699 (v.2), f. 189v

Each one of the 14 main divisions in the manuscript features a lavishly illuminated frontispiece. The splendid leaf shown here opens the 10th book in Moses Maimonides' Code, *Sefer Tohorah* (Book of Cleanliness), which discusses the laws of purity. The fan-tailed peacock in the lower border is a frequently encountered motif in manuscripts from the Portuguese school of Hebrew illumination. But this manuscript stands out from other products of the Portuguese school in its decorative style, which is particularly Italianate. It also differs in its contents, being neither a bible nor a liturgy, but a legal code.

Exhibited here is the stunning introduction to Maimonides' 13th book, *Sefer Mishpatim* (Book of Civil Laws), covering the law of employment, debt and inheritance. The exquisite mauve and red tracery, luxurious floriated mounts and burnished gold lettering are distinctive hallmarks of Hebrew manuscripts created in Lisbon during the last quarter of the 15th century. Undoubtedly this sumptuous codex was decorated in the same atelier that produced the famed Lisbon Bible and various other accomplished specimens. About 30 Hebrew manuscripts survive from the Lisbon workshop, which operated between 1469 and 1496, this one being the earliest dated amongst them.

102 Book of Civil Laws
Lisbon Maimonides
Legal Code in two volumes
Lisbon, Portugal
1471–72
332 x 240 mm
MS Harley MS 5699 (v.2), f. 355v

103 Frontispiece to *Orah Hayim*
Legal Code of Jacob ben Asher
in two volumes
Italy
1475
350 x 265 mm
MS Harley 5716 (v.1), f. 8r

The *Arba'ah Turim* (The Four Rows) is the title of a 14th-century legal Code authored by the rabbinic scholar Jacob ben Asher of Toledo (1270–1340). Shown here is the beginning of the Code's first division, *Orah Hayim* (Path of Life), covering the laws of worship and ritual observance, from a 15th-century Italian manuscript. The scribe, Hayim Barbut, who may have come from Spain, exhibits a beautiful semi-cursive Sephardi hand. The exquisite Ferrarese-style border shielding the text combines florid motifs with animals, birds, vases and cherubs. The coat-of-arms in the lower margin belongs to Yoav Emmanuel, the patron of two manuscripts seen earlier (*figs.* 59–60, 63–4).

This miniature of Adam and Eve in the Garden of Eden is the only one in the manuscript related directly to the text. It illustrates the verse inscribed in the upper-left panel, 'It is not good that the man should be alone, I will make him a helpmate...' (Genesis 2:18). The verse opens a discussion in *Even ha-'Ezer* (Stone of Help), a section in ben Asher's Code on family law. Unusually, the protagonists' nakedness is covered by foliate girdles rather than fig leaves. Note the human-faced serpent – a motif borrowed from Christian art – coiled around the Tree of Knowledge. The codex was still in Italy in the early 17th century, as attested by four censorial notes dated between 1598 and 1610.

104 Adam and Eve
Legal Code of Jacob ben Asher in two volumes
Italy
1475
350 x 265 mm
MS Harley 5717 (v. 2), f. 5v

105 Frontispiece to *Hoshen Mishpat*
Legal Code of Jacob ben Asher
Germany
1360
205 x 150 mm
MS Add. 27137, f. 14r (detail)

The scribe Yehudah bar Yosef Arama completed this manuscript in 1360 for Gershom ben Yekuthiel. The text comes from the fourth division of Jacob ben Asher's Code, the *Hoshen Mishpat* (Shield of Judgement), which covers civil and criminal law, including finance and torts. The tripartite illustration shown here, which decorates the frontispiece, reflects the legal subject of the work. In the centre, for instance, the bearded figure, seen conversing, might represent Rabbi Simeon ben Galili, whose name appears in the opening line. The left-hand miniature shows two men counting money watched by onlookers, while on the right bystanders witness one man beating up another.

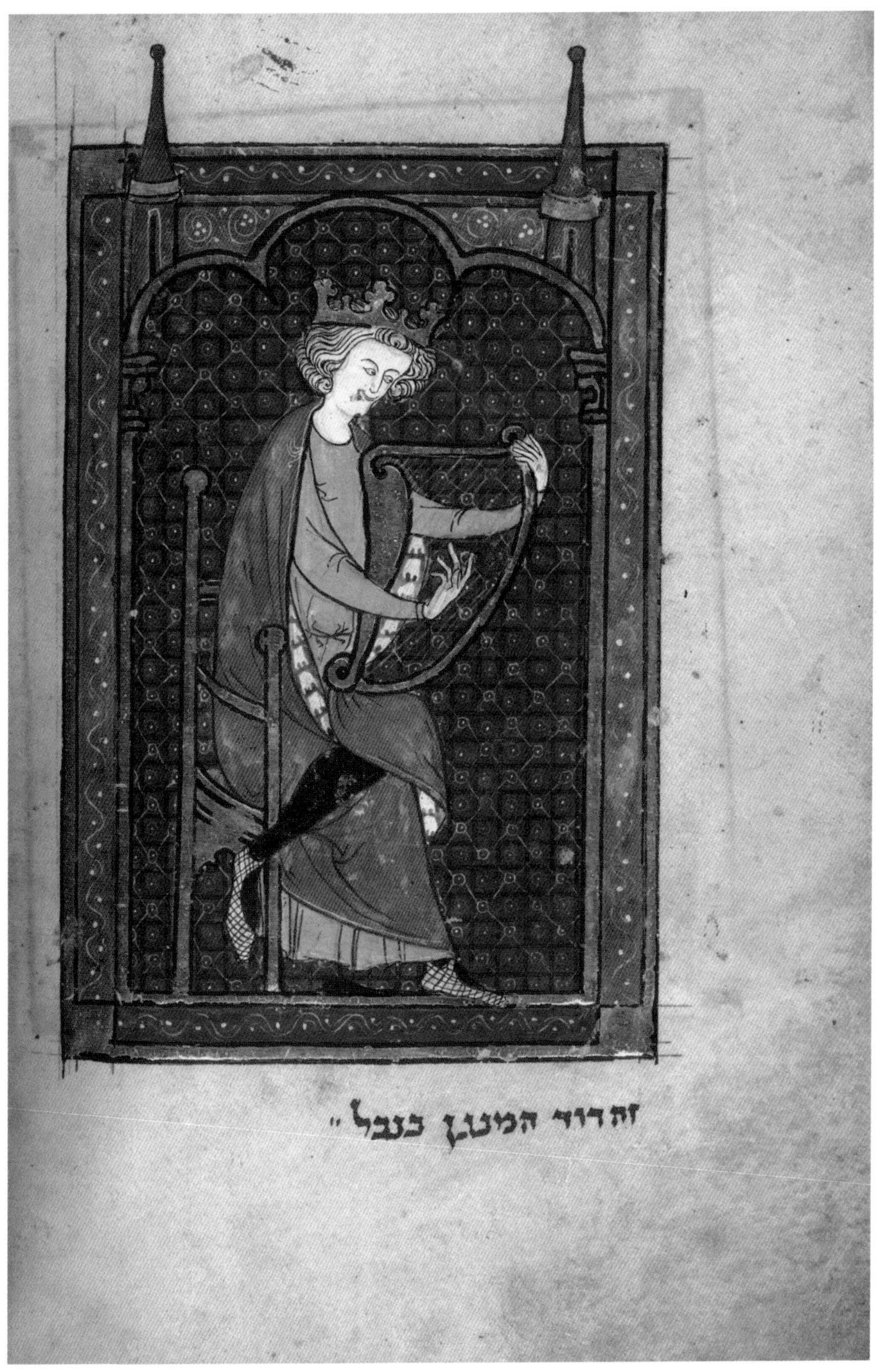

A popular character in Jewish and Christian art, King David appears in countless manuscripts as a shepherd, warrior or, as seen here, as a gifted musician. This full-page miniature shows him crowned, wearing a bright orange-red gown lined with royal ermine. Seated cross-legged in a golden chair, he is harping. The architectural setting suggests a royal residence. The Miscellany contains 49 full-page miniatures displaying biblical characters and narratives, which were executed by Christian illuminators attached to three major contemporary Parisian workshops. The iconography draws on imagery found in contemporary *Bibles moralisées*.

106 King David the musician
North French Hebrew Miscellany
France
c. 1278–98
165 x 125 mm
MS Add. 11639, f. 117v

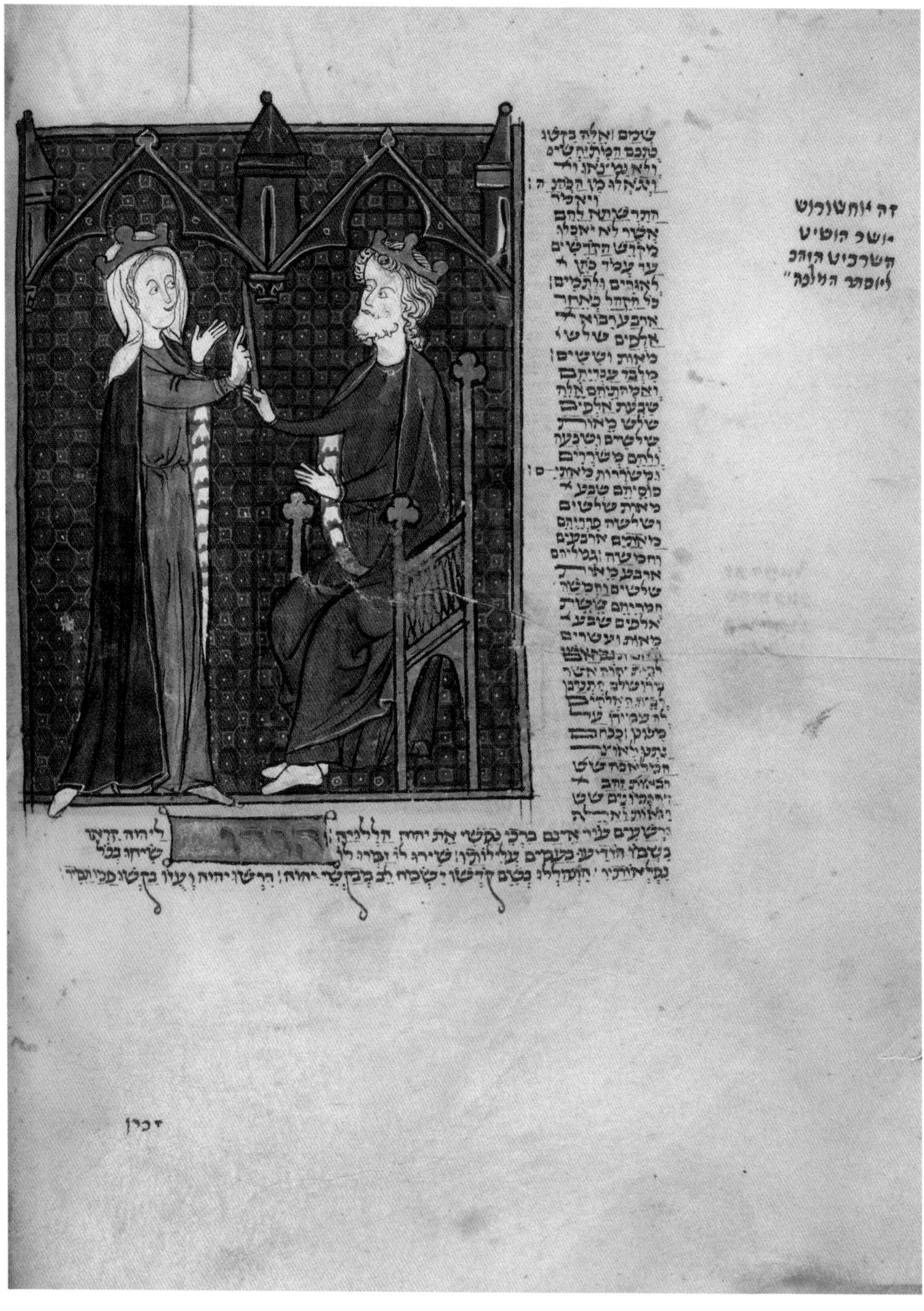

107 Esther and King Ahasuerus
North French Hebrew Miscellany
France
c. 1278–98
165 x 125 mm
MS Add. 11639, f. 260v

In this French miniature Queen Esther finds favour before King Ahasuerus, illustrating the verse, '...and the King held out to Esther the golden sceptre...' (Esther 5:2). Both figures are crowned, and clad in robes garnished with blue and white ermine. Details, such as the delicate facial expressions, the king's wavy hair and the folds in the gowns, reveal the work of a competent artist who painted in the sophisticated French Gothic style of the period. The lattice work and trefoil finials decorating the chair and the skilfully designed backdrop attest further to a high level of craftsmanship. Typically Gothic, also, is the miniature's diapered surfaces in magenta and blue.

Eighty-four different groups of texts, including hundreds of poems, were copied in this unrivalled manuscript. It contains the Pentateuch, the prophetical readings and the liturgy for the entire year. It also includes the earliest complete Hebrew version of Tobit. Although the scribe's name, Benjamin, appears four times in the manuscript, the lack of a proper colophon means that virtually nothing is known about either the scribe's or the patron's identities. This led to the assumption that Benjamin the Scribe wrote the Miscellany for personal use. The three-headed dragon and the *fauvel* (horse from hell) in this ornate scribal note were probably modelled on monsters in a bestiary.

108 Benjamin the Scribe
North French Hebrew Miscellany
France
c. 1278–98
165 x 125 mm
MS Add. 11639, f. 306v

109 Mythical bird
North French Hebrew Miscellany
France
c. 1278–98
165 x 125 mm
MS Add. 11639, f. 517v

Painted on a tessellated red surface inside a gold-framed roundel is the mythical bird *Bar-Yokhani* or *Ziz*, possibly inspired by a prototype in a contemporary bestiary. A symbol of Messianic hope and aspiration, the *Bar-Yokhani* features mostly in manuscripts from the 13th to 15th centuries from Ashkenaz (Franco-German lands). According to the midrash (running commentaries on the Pentateuch and other parts of the Hebrew Bible), it is one of the creatures that will be consumed by the just and the righteous at the Messianic banquet in the world to come.

זה עץ בתוך התיבה' והיונה עליו נחה

In this miniature of Noah's ark, the ark, shaped like a house with a brick base and two windows, is surrounded by choppy green waves. Unusually, Mount Ararat, where Noah's ark came to rest (Genesis 8:4–12), is not shown. The only sign that the waters had somewhat receded is the tree on the left of the illustration, and the dove returning to Noah with an olive leaf in its beak. The raven which, according to the biblical story, flew to and fro until it found dry land, is shown perched on the roof of the ark. According to scholars, this illustration of Noah's ark is unique in Ashkenazi manuscripts of that period.

110 Noah's Ark
North French Hebrew Miscellany
France
c. 1278–98
165 x 125 mm
MS Add. 11639, f. 521r

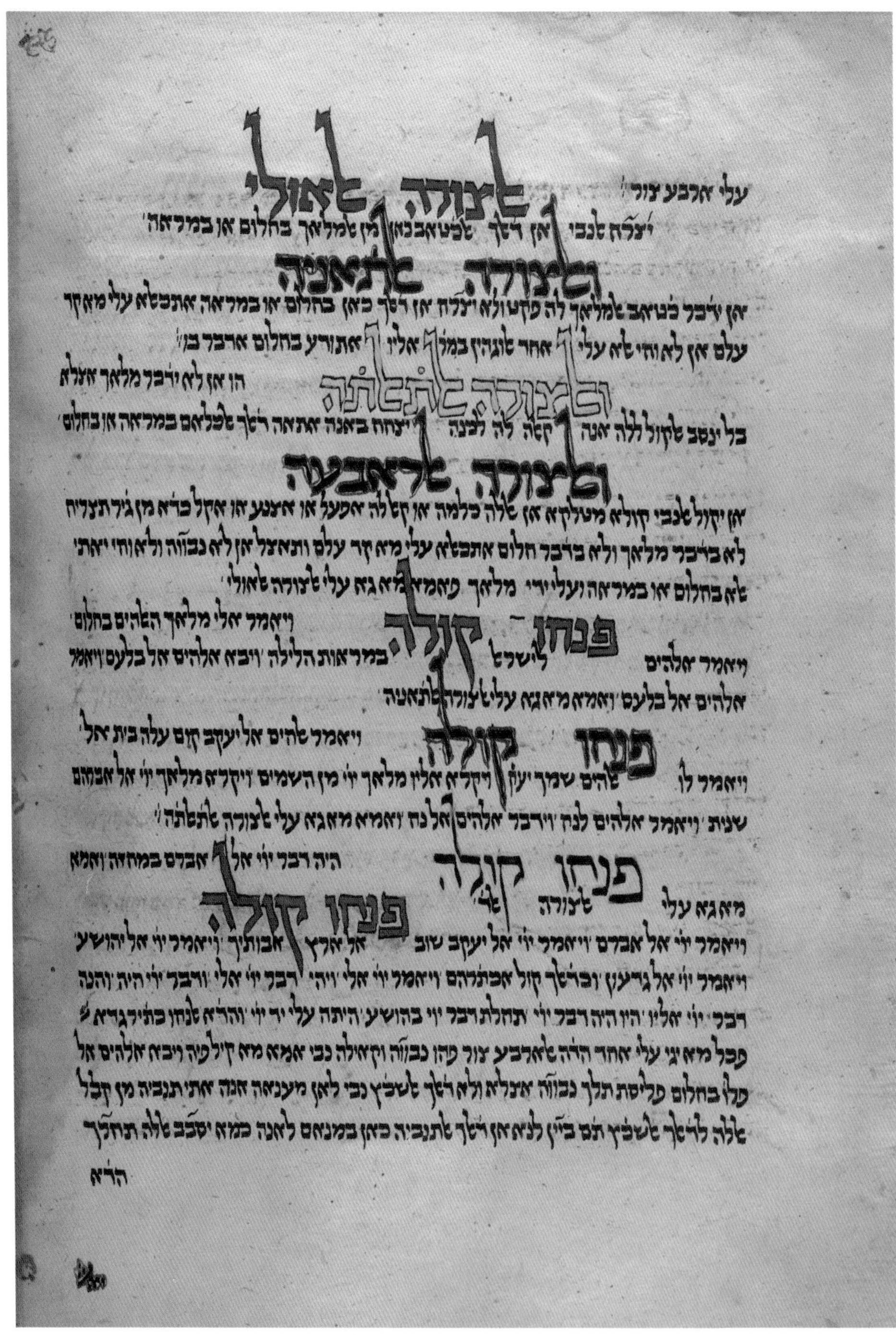

111 Decorated script
Maimonides' *Guide for the Perplexed*
Tawila, Yemen
1380
345 x 240 mm
MS I.O. ISL 3679, f. 107v

Maimonides completed *Moreh Nevukhin* (Guide for the Perplexed), his greatest philosophical masterpiece, in Egypt in 1190. This leaf derives from the earliest known complete copy of the work in the Judeo-Arabic original (Arabic in Hebrew script). Penned in Yemen in 1380 by Shalom ben Ezra al-'Anasi, the manuscript's visual appeal stems solely from its immaculate calligraphy and coloured letters and words. Kept in Yemen for 500 years, it was deposited in 1877 in the India Office Library by Lord Northbrook (1826–1904), grandson of Sir Thomas Baring (1772–1848), who received it from Joseph Wolff (1795–1862), a Christian missionary of German-Jewish descent.

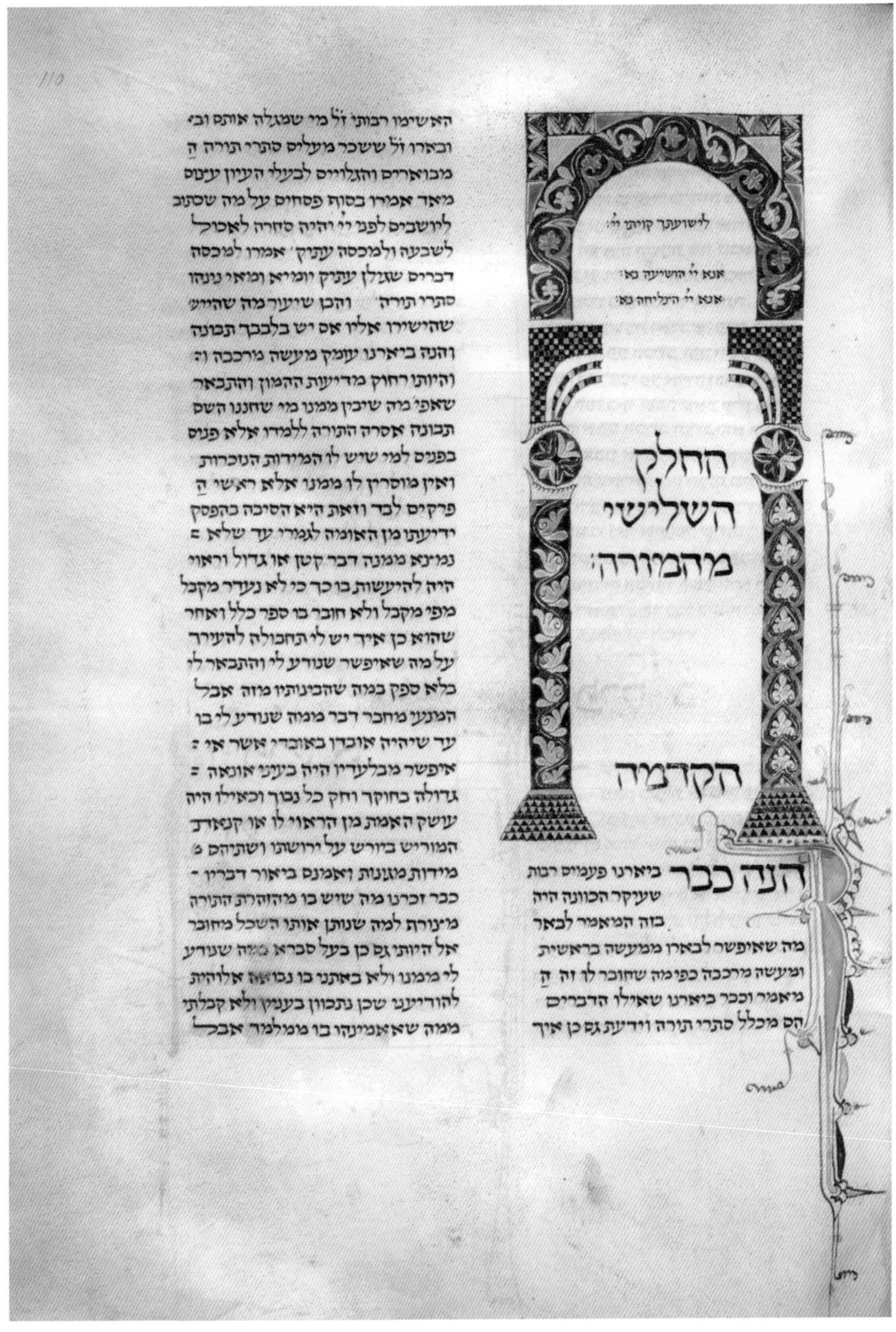

The main decorative elements in this copy of Maimonides' *Guide for the Perplexed* are the penwork embellishments and colourful arcades placed at the start of each main section. This incipit page has an ornate arcade painted in a French Gothic style that was fashionable in 13th-century Rome. An unknown artist from a Roman workshop executed the decorations. Rome is also where Shabetai ben Mattatya, a wealthy banker and the patron of the manuscript lived, pointing further to the codex's origins. The pseudonym in the colophon is the scribe's, Avraham ben Yom Tov Hacohen, who between 1284 and 1290 copied four additional manuscripts, two of them for the same patron.

112 French-Gothic arcades
Moses Maimonides' *Guide for the Perplexed*
Rome?, Italy
1283
305 x 215 mm
MS Harley 7586A, f. 110r

113 Royal coat of arms
Maimonides' *Guide for the Perplexed*
Catalonia, Spain
c. 1350
300 x 200 mm
MS Or. 14061, f. 156v

This 14th-century illuminated codex of Maimonides' *Guide for the Perplexed* was probably intended for the library of the kings of Castile and Leon. Among its 200 or more illuminations is this panel decorated with a crowned gold lion rampant beneath a Moorish arch, representing the Spanish royal coat-of-arms. Although unsigned, the codex was probably copied by Levi ben Isaac Caro of Salamanca, whereas the decorations have been attributed to the school of Ferrer Bassa, a well-known Catalan court painter.

This exquisitely designed page combines illuminated word panels and luxuriant extensions rendered in dazzling pigments and gold. Levi ben Isaac Caro of Salamanca, the scribe believed to have copied the manuscript, exhibits an elegant semi-cursive Sephardi hand. At one time in the possession of the court physician of the Ottoman sultan Abdul Hamid II, the manuscript was last owned by David Solomon Sassoon (1882–1942), one of the greatest Jewish bibliophiles of modern times.

114 Decorated introductory panels
Maimonides' *Guide for the Perplexed*
Catalonia, Spain
c. 1350
300 x 200 mm
MS Or. 14061, f. 89r

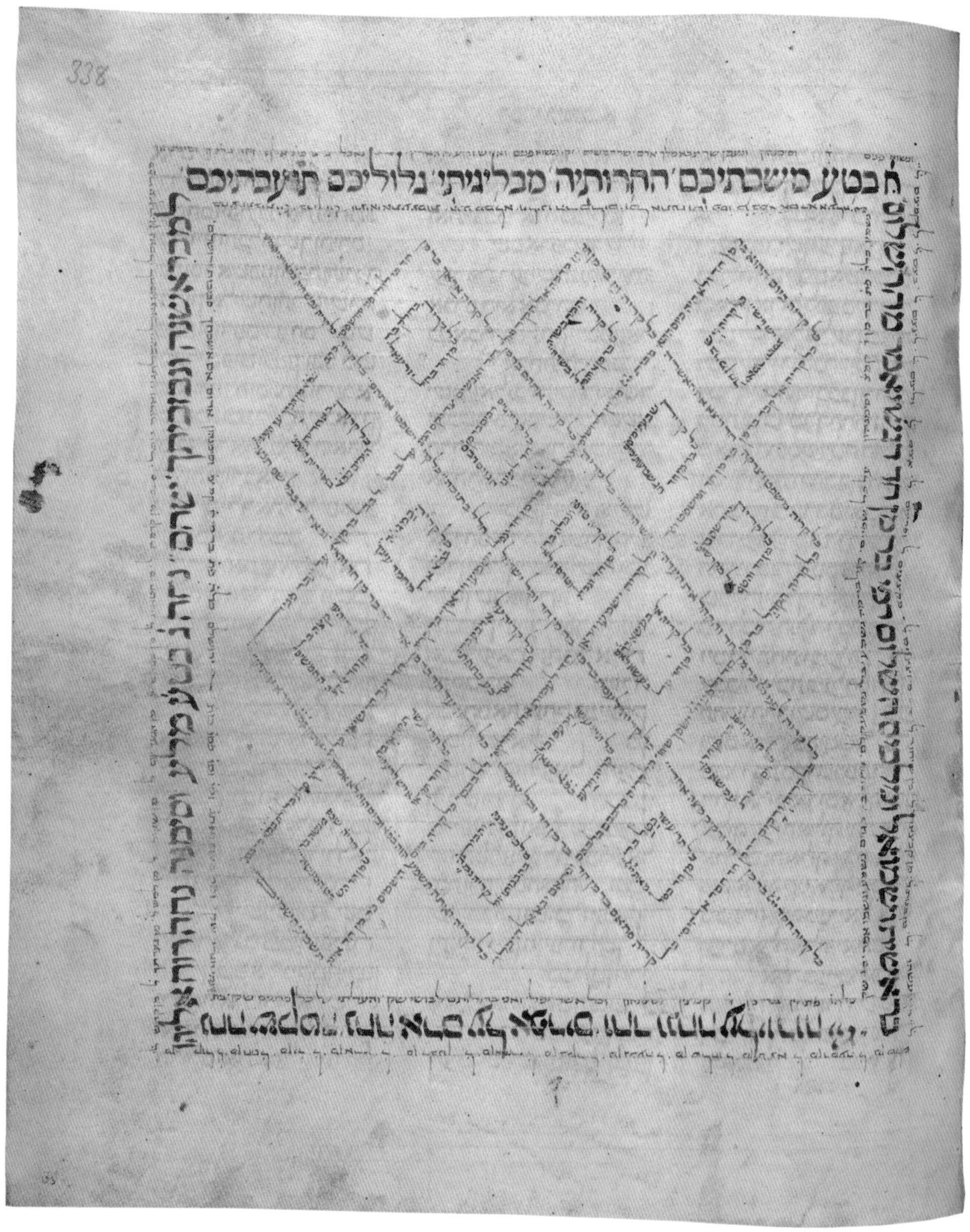

115 Micrographic carpet page
First Ibn Merwas Bible
Masoretic Bible
Toledo, Spain
1300
185 x 170 mm
MS OR. 2201, f. 338r

Six carpet-pages of micrographic *Masorah* framed by inscriptions are included in this codex, handwritten by the copyist Joseph ben Judah Ibn Marvas for a patron whose name has long been erased. Typical of the manuscript are its geometrical designs outlined in minuscule lettering, as illustrated by this page covered with a trellis pattern made of lozenges.

The two text columns shown here are enclosed by stylish micrography fusing abstract and heraldic elements. The crested helmets (in the upper margin) and *fleurs-de-lis* motifs are particularly striking. Interestingly, in this codex both the *Masorah Magna* (notes added in the upper and lower margins) and the *Masorah Parva* (penned between the columns) were outlined in micrography. The scribe Ezra ben Jacob ben Aderet copied the scriptural text, but another unnamed copyist might have devised the elaborate micrographic designs. As often happened in medieval Hebrew manuscripts, the scribe would usually sign the colophon relegating other contributors to anonymity.

116 Opening to Hosea
Prophets and Hagiographa in two volumes
Castellon d'Ampurias, Spain
1396
240 x 175 mm
MS Harley 5774 (v.1), f. 288v

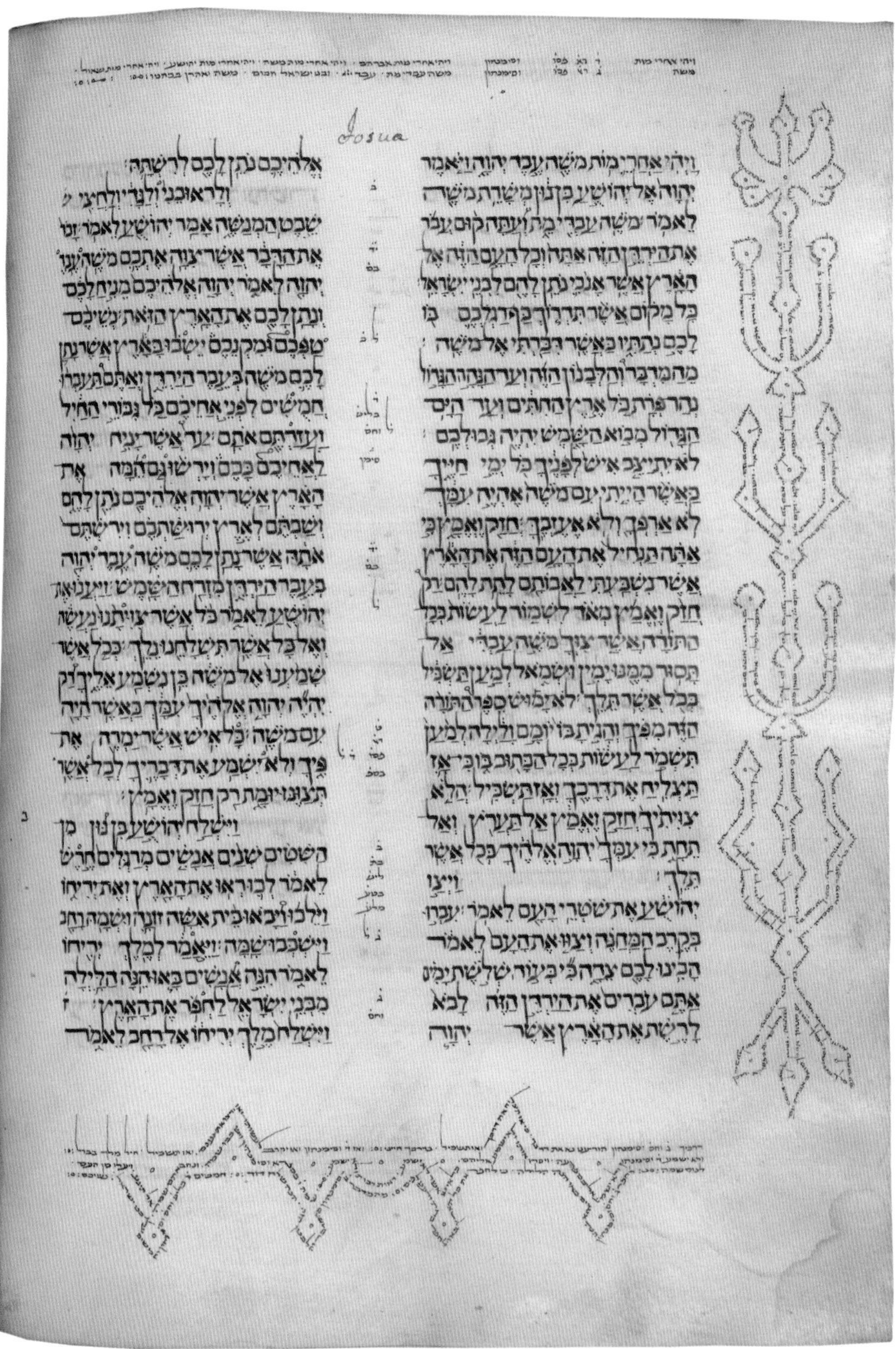

117 Opening to Joshua
London Catalan Bible
Catalonia, Spain
third quarter of 14th century
305 x 225 mm
MS Add. 15252, f. 116v

In this codex (as in *figs.* 115–22), micrographic *Masorah* constitutes the sole decorative element. Geometrical and abstract patterns in microscopic script adorn many of its leaves. Note the charming candelabrum-tree displayed in the margin. Details about the scribe, patron and the fate of the codex after completion remain obscure until the 16th century when it became the property of Samuel ben Moses de Medina, a Talmudist from Salonica. In 1618 the codex was in Italy, where the censor Giovanni Domenico Caretto, who operated mainly in Mantua, revised it. Its last owner was the Duke of Sussex, whose Hebrew manuscripts were acquired by the British Museum in 1844.

There is a striking resemblance between the ornamental micrography in this codex and that of the Castellon d'Ampurias manuscript shown earlier (*fig.* 115). It is quite possible that both were parts of the same Hebrew Bible, which at some point seems to have been split up. An inscription dated 1678, once attached to the original binding, now lost, suggests a similar explanation. As this opening shows, here too, both types of *Masorah* have been used in the micrographic patterning. The text laid out like a wall of brick contains the last part of the *Song of the Sea*, a triumphant ode extolling God's attributes, which Moses and the Israelites sang after crossing the Red Sea (Exodus 15: 1–18).

118 First song of Moses
London Catalan Pentateuch
Catalonia, Spain
late 14th century
220 x 170 mm
MS Harley 5773, f. 56r

119 End of Ruth
Pentateuch with prophetical readings,
France or Germany
13th–14th century
380 x 285 mm
MS Add. 21160, f. 300v

This leaf adorned with intricate micrographic designs ranks among the most magnificent examples of Hebrew manuscript art. The masoretic annotations are fashioned into an elaborate border composed of architectural structures, lush vegetal scrolls and mythical beasts. Penned inside the frame, in a handsome Ashkenazi square hand, is the final section from the biblical Book of Ruth (Ruth 4:13–22), which provides the lineage of King David.

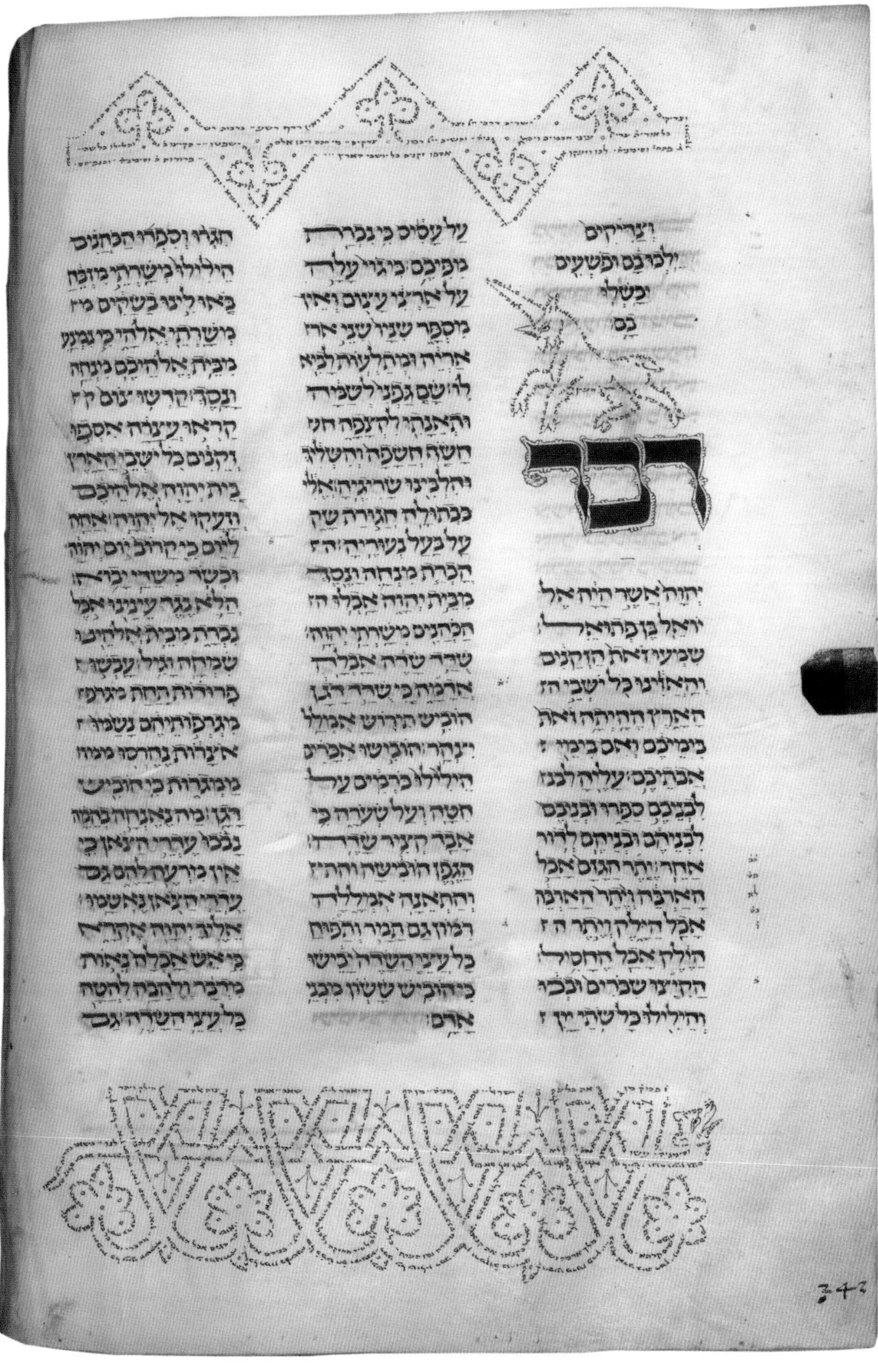

The opening word of Joel is prominently displayed on this page in large ornamental characters. Eye-catching micrographic designs include a unicorn and tracery combining vegetal, abstract and heraldic motifs. Note the monster's head and tail emerging from the dainty filigree in the lower margin. This manuscript provides remarkable examples of micrography, an expression of Jewish art dating back to the Middle Ages and still practised today. The scribe's dexterity in visually manipulating the masoretic notation erupts in a Gothic display of abstract and animate shapes. These elements prevailed in Franco-German manuscripts of the 13th to 15th centuries.

120 Opening to Joel
Prophets and Hagiographa
probably Germany
13th century
435 x 320 mm
MS Or. 2091, f. 243v

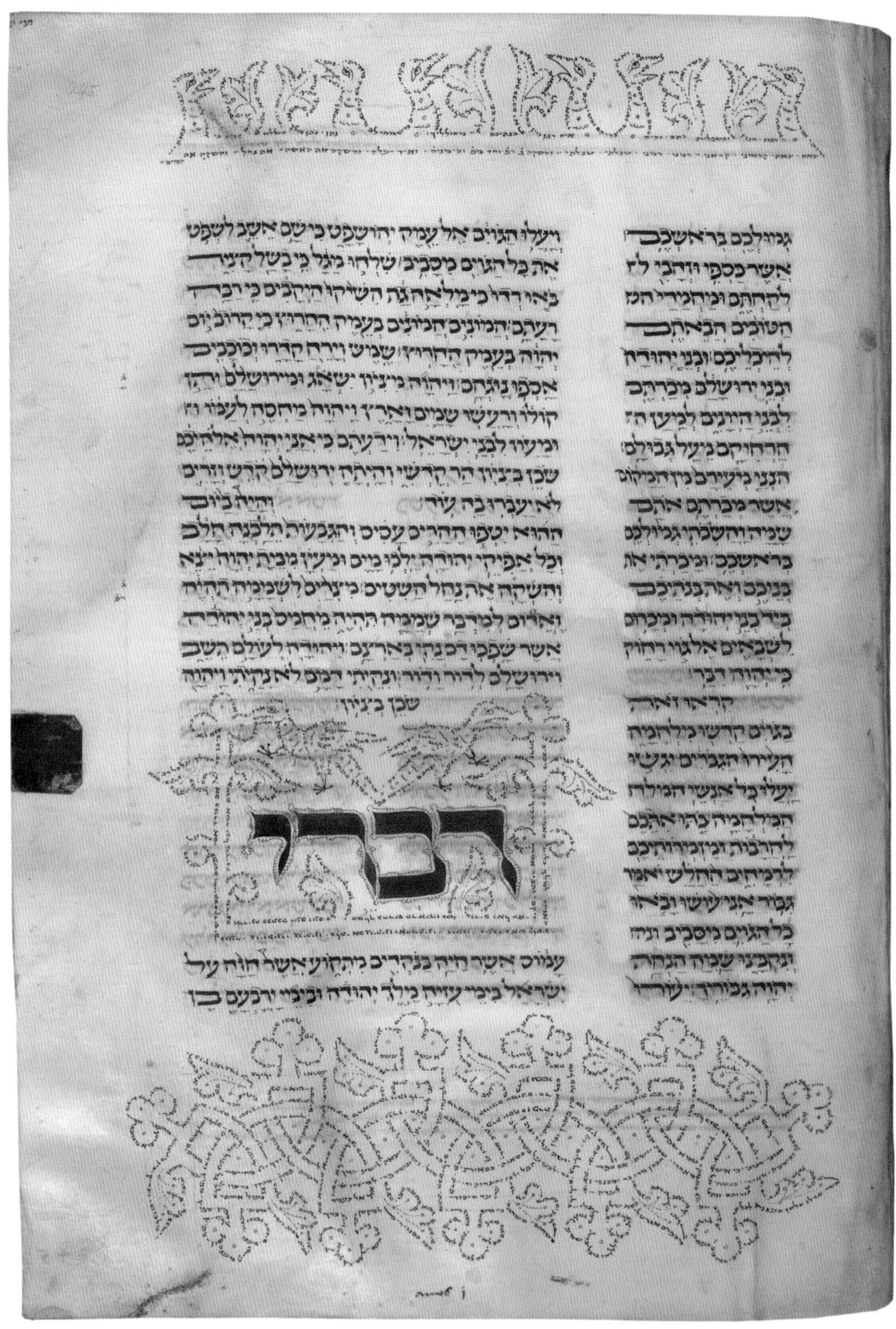

121 Opening to Amos
Prophets and Hagiographa
probably Germany
13th century
435 x 320 mm
MS Or. 2091, f. 245r

Initially scribes employed text from the *Masorah* to devise micrographic patterns, but with time they began utilizing other sources, particularly the Hebrew Bible. For example, verses from the Proverbs and Psalms were often fashioned in micrography. In this opening to Amos, the anonymous scribe enclosed the first word *Divre* (the words of) within a micrographic panel composed of foliage and fabulous creatures. A row of birds' heads in profile and a magnificent floral interlace adorn the upper and lower margins of the page.

This splendid leaf, coming from the same manuscript as that shown opposite, again demonstrates the scribe's consummate mastery in shaping the masoretic notation into micrographic embellishments. Adorning the opening word to Proverbs is a pair of dragons with intertwined tails. Below the columns of text the scribe has constructed a micrographic web of foliage, rosettes and interlocking Stars of David. Another interesting feature of this large-size codex is its stamped vellum binding embellished with brass clasps, corners and bosses. The binding bears the date 1524, but the place of its production is unknown.

122 Opening to Proverbs
Prophets and Hagiographa
probably Germany
13th century
435 x 320 mm
MS Or. 2091, f. 324r

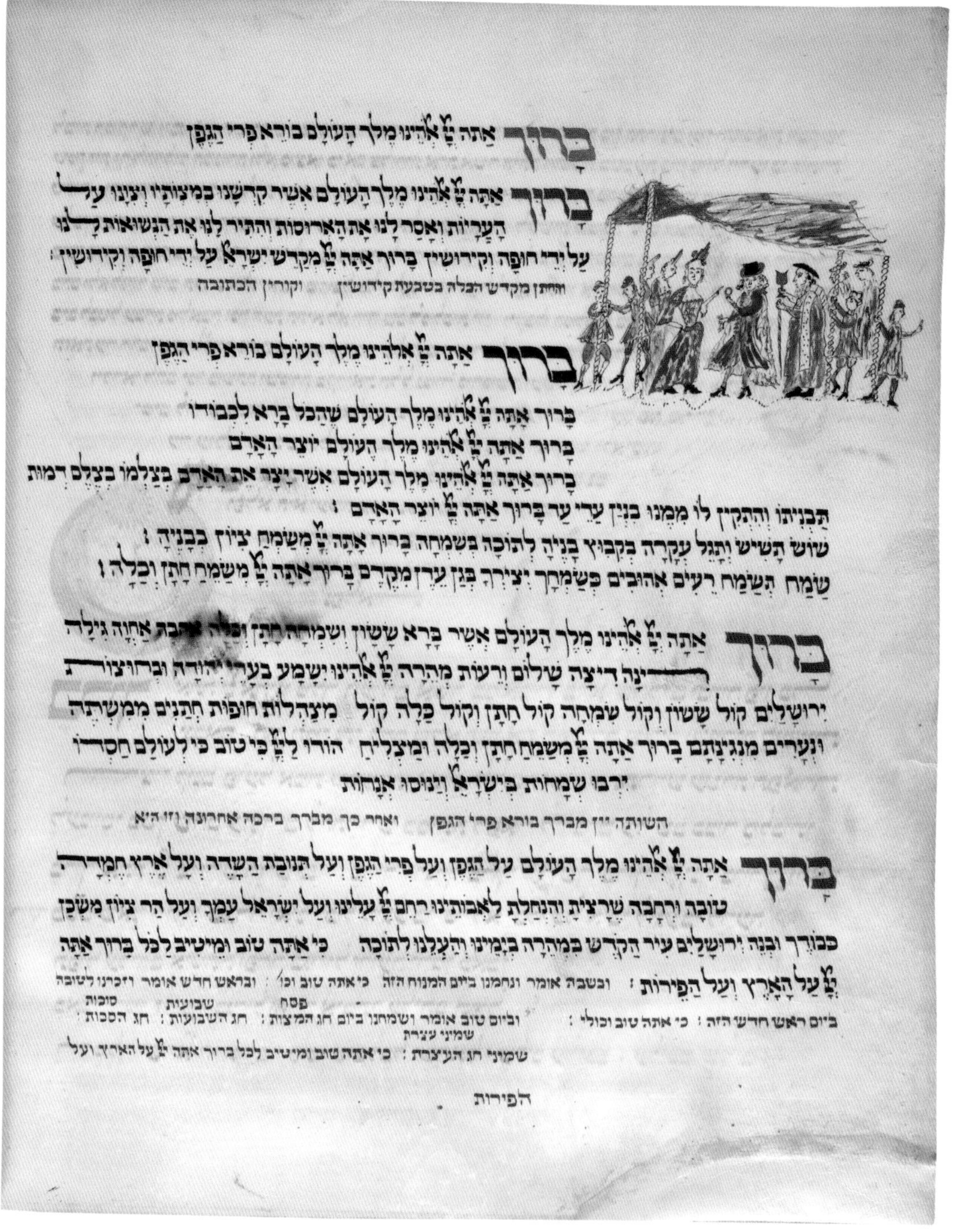

123 Jewish wedding
Liturgical selections and Tobit
London?
1714
380 x 295 mm
MS Harley 5713, f. 17v

In this wedding scene the humour lies in the bride's casual demeanour under the ritual canopy. With right hand on hip, she raises her left hand, pointing a finger as the groom prepares to place the ring on it while reciting the betrothal formula. The groom's livery and cloak with ruff, and the women's *fontanges* (headdresses) provide valuable examples of 18th-century European Jewish dress. Penned in Hebrew calligraphic square script are blessings recited during the ceremony. Instructions for the order of service have been inserted in smaller red script. Aaron ben Moses of Novogrodek wrote this manuscript for Humphrey Wanley, librarian to Robert Harley, Earl of Oxford.

This page introduces a series of poetical pieces peculiar to the Ashkenazi rite (from Franco-German lands) known as *Yotserot*, which are usually recited during the morning prayers on Sabbaths and other special occasions. It comes from a finely crafted manuscript, with its calligraphy modelled on the Hebrew Amsterdam typefaces which, at the time, were very trendy in both manuscripts and printed books. Above and below the decorated title panel are pen and ink illustrations showing Moses on Mount Sinai receiving the Tablets of the Law (top), and Adam and Eve with the serpent (bottom). The pictures in the manuscript emulate imagery in contemporary printed books.

124 Beginning of special prayers
Prayer book with poetical pieces
Vienna
1720
290 x 230 mm
MS Add. 17867, f. 84v

125–126 Scenes from Joshua
Fathnama
Biblical paraphrase
Isfahan?, Persia
end of 17th or beginning of 18th century
290 x 200 mm
MS Or. 13704, ff. 31v-32r

Fathnama (Book of Conquest) is essentially a poetical paraphrase by the Jewish Persian poet Imrani of Shiraz (1454–1536) of narratives from Joshua, Ruth and Samuel. Imrani strove to elevate the biblical tale to the standard of the Persian epic, and his works combine Jewish and Muslim legendary material and literary elements. These striking miniatures, which draw on Persian imagery, portray events from Joshua. They belong to a *Fathnama* manuscript that was produced around 1700. Since God forbade Moses to set foot in the Promised Land, Joshua led the Israelites in the conquest of Canaan.

The scene above, depicting the capture of the city of Jericho, shows seven priests encircling the town's walls and blowing on rams' horns (Joshua 6). The image opposite, depicting Joshua on horseback, brandishing a javelin and surrounded by warriors, probably illustrates the fierce battle for the Amorite city of Ai (Joshua 8: 18–26). The text of this beautifully wrought Judeo-Persian manuscript (Persian in Hebrew characters) was penned in a semi-cursive Hebrew script by several unidentified copyists. The manuscript formerly belonged in David Solomon Sassoon's collection and was acquired by the British Library in 1975.

רַגְלַי מִדֶּחִי : אֶתְהַלֵּךְ לִפְנֵי יְיָ   פֵּרוּשׁ אברבנל
בְּאַרְצוֹת הַחַיִּים : הֶאֱמַנְתִּי כִּי
אֲדַבֵּר אֲנִי עָנִיתִי מְאֹד :   אֲנִי
אָמַרְתִּי בְחָפְזִי כָּל הָאָדָם
כּוֹזֵב

127 King David at prayer
The Leipnik *Hagadah*
Service book for Passover eve
Altona, Denmark?
1740
MS Sloane 3173, f. 27r

Dressed in regal finery King David is illustrated kneeling in prayer. The lyre and the book of Psalms before him allude to his fame as a musician and psalmist. The illustrations in this beautifully wrought Passover service book were modelled on copperplate engravings in the 1695 and 1712 printed editions of the Amsterdam *Hagadah*. The Leipnik *Hagadah* was created by Joseph ben David Leipnik, an influential Moravian scribe-artist active in Hamburg and Altona, who, between 1731 and 1740, crafted 13 other *Hagadot*. It is also called the Sloane *Hagadah* after its former owner, Sir Hans Sloane (1660–1753), who is regarded as the founder of the British Museum.

The Holy City of Jerusalem, depicted as a prosperous 18th-century European town with beautiful edifices and dwellings, seems dwarfed by the imposing baroque Temple, its tower crowned by the Star of David. This miniature accompanies the Passover hymn *Adir Hu* ('Strong is He'), which extols the attributes of the Creator and expresses the centuries-long Jewish yearning to restore Jerusalem and its holy Sanctuary. The Leipnik *Hagadah* reflects Joseph ben David Leipnik's innovative artistry and provides a valuable example of 18th-century Hebrew manuscript art.

128 Jerusalem and the Temple
The Leipnik *Hagadah*
Service book for Passover eve
Altona, Denmark?
1740
MS Sloane 3173, f. 34r

129 Frontispiece to *Hagadah*
Service book for Passover eve
Hamburg and Altona
1740
230 x 165 mm
MS Add. 18724, f. 1r

Beneath a medallion showing King David harping appear the figures of Moses (right) and Aaron (left). Moses carries a staff and the Tablets of the Law, while Aaron, dressed in the vestments of the High Priest, holds a censor. This composition typifies almost all the title pages of *Hagadot* produced by Jacob ben Judah Leib of Berlin, and is based on printed models, particularly the 1712 edition of the Amsterdam *Hagadah*. At least 27 of the manuscripts that were copied and painted by this scribe-illuminator between 1718–41 have survived. Born probably in Berlin, he spent most of his artistic career in Hamburg and Altona, where he occasionally worked on commission for wealthy patrons.

The captioned miniature above depicts Moses and Aaron performing miracles in front of Pharaoh in an attempt to persuade the latter to free the Hebrew slaves (Exodus 7:8-10). The scribe Jacob ben Judah Leib of Berlin shows a grasp of perspective and skill in portraying human figures, some drawn in profile. The palatial décor and the vibrant colours evoke Joseph Leipnik's style (*figs.* 127–28). The latter had apparently exerted a considerable influence on Jacob of Berlin's work which, despite its attraction, lacks the charming freshness of Leipnik's style. The calligraphy, especially the semi-cursive script reserved for Abrabanel's commentary, is quite remarkable.

130 Moses and Aaron at Pharaoh's court
Service book for Passover eve
Hamburg and Altona
1740
230 x 165 mm
MS Add. 18724, f. 15v

131 The Song of the Birds
Perek Shirah
Chapter of Song in Hebrew and Yiddish
Vienna or Pressburg
c. 1740
130 x 80 mm
MS Or. 12983, f. 8v

The illustrated pages above and opposite contain the text of *Perek Shirah* (Chapter of Song), a cosmic hymn of praise in which every created thing, from the animate to the celestial, thanks the Creator for its continuing existence. The praises are mostly biblical verses, the greater part of them being citations from Psalms. The earliest extant versions of the work date from the 10th century. In this version the divine creations are divided into five chapters. This fine miniature, opening the chapter on birds depicts some of the domestic and wild birds mentioned in the text.

The illustration here, from the same *Perek Shirah* seen opposite, illustrates the chapter on the four-footed beasts and shows 13 different animals, not all identifiable. Although the manuscript is unsigned, the calligraphy and style of illumination are typical of the work of Aaron Wolf Herlingen of Gewitsch.

A gifted Moravian copyist-miniaturist, he was active between 1724–52, creating several dozen delightful manuscripts, many of which have survived. Considered as the most prolific scribe-artist of the 18th-century Moravian school, Aaron Wolf Herlingen of Gewitsch was equally its most talented calligrapher and penman.

132 The Song of the Animals
Perek Shirah
Chapter of Song in Hebrew and Yiddish
Vienna or Pressburg
c. 1740
130 x 80 mm
MS Or. 12983, f. 12v

133 Italian *Ketubah*
Marriage contract
Modena, Italy
1 October 1557 (*sic* 21 October 1757)
700 x 590 mm
MS Or. 6706

A mandatory contract given to a Jewish bride on her wedding day, the *Ketubah* is intended to safeguard her rights should the marriage break up. Besides the monetary stipulations, it provides the couple's names and the date and place of the wedding ceremony. This elaborate contract between Ephraim ben Kalonymus Sanguini and Luna bat Mordecai Faro features an architectural structure surmounted by cherubs bearing trumpets. The outer borders include micrographic interlacing, the signs of the zodiac and biblical vignettes to the Sabbath readings following the wedding. Perhaps in an attempt to increase its value, the contract's original date of 1757 was changed to 1557.

Decorated with colourful tempera roses and flowers, this contract records the betrothal of Moses, son of Samuel, and Rachel, daughter of Abraham, at Eupatoria in 1842. As is customary in Karaite marriage contracts, the text is in Hebrew rather than Aramaic, and the name of the ruler of the land – Emperor Nicolai I – is inscribed in large red square characters on the document, evidently in an attempt to show the Karaites' obedience to him.

134 Karaite *Ketubah*
Marriage contract
Eupatoria
1842
750 x 580 mm
MS Or. 15685

135 Indian *Ketubah*
Marriage contract
Calcutta, India
1888
595 x 350 mm
MS Or. 15651

This marriage contract records the betrothal of Yaakov Hai Yosef Avraham Ta'azi and Simhah bat Natan Yosef Douwek ha-Cohen, in Calcutta in 1888. The rampant tigers, representing Indian fauna, and the silvery fish, symbolizing fertility, are decorative motifs specifically associated with contracts created for the Baghdadis of India. Formerly in the library of the illustrious bibliophile David Solomon Sassoon, this contract was added to the British Library collections in 2000.

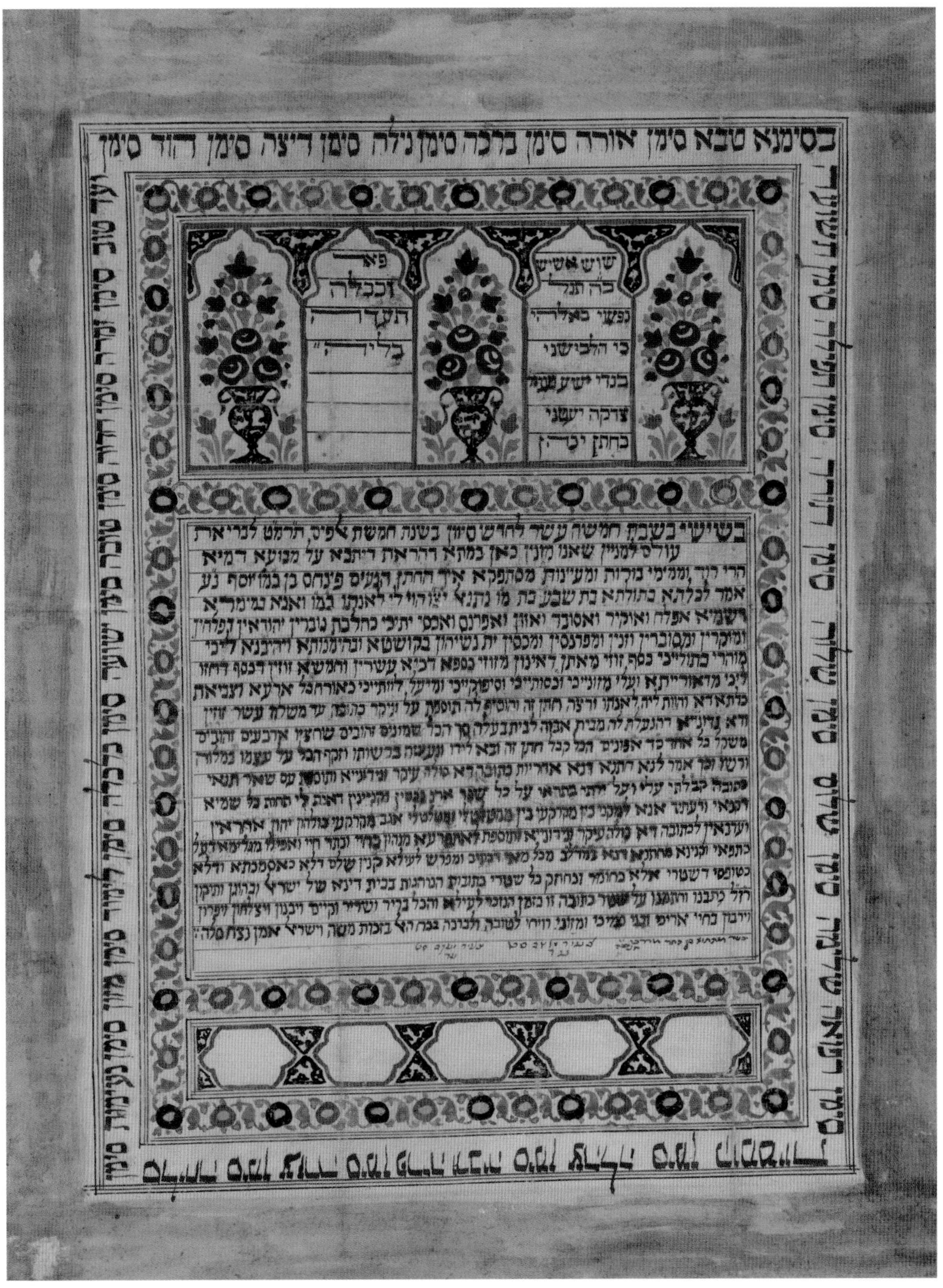
בסימנא טבא סימן אורה סימן ברכה סימן גילה סימן דיצה סימן הוד סימן

שוש אשיש בה׳ תגל נפשי באלהי כי הלבישני בגדי ישע מעיל צדקה יעטני כחתן יכהן

פאר וככלה תעדה כליה

The *Ketubah* deed has a history stretching back 2000 years, making it one of the earliest documents granting women legal and financial rights. The traditional text, which has remained unchanged for centuries, is written in Aramaic (a Semitic language related to Hebrew). It is customary to read the text of the *Ketubah* to the couple under the bridal canopy during the marriage ceremony. This contract records the marriage of Pinhas, son of Yosef, to Bat-Sheva‘, daughter of Netan'el, in Herat in 1889. Islamic and Persian elements can be detected in the decoration, which is typical of 19th-century Jewish marriage contracts from that area.

136 Afghani *Ketubah*
Marriage contract
Herat, Afghanistan
1889
590 x 380 mm
MS Or. 15893

137–138 Marelli's Scroll
Scroll of Esther
Italy
c. 1573
c. 2100 x 165 mm
(length and height of entire scroll)
MS Or. 13028

The biblical Book of Esther (*Megilat Esther*) tells of how the Jewish maiden Esther secured the deliverance of her people in Persia from Haman's death decree, during the reign of King Ahasuerus, Xerex of Persia (486–65 BC). These events are commemorated every year in the synagogue during the feast of *Purim* (Festival of Lots), when a reading of Esther is made from a plain, unadorned parchment scroll. The practice of embellishing the borders of Esther scrolls produced for home reading emerged, apparently, in Italy in the second half of the 16th-century. The imagery in this scroll bears no relation to the Esther story related within its borders, which are filled with an

extravagant array of *putti*, grotesques, telamons, fauns and pagan goddesses bearing heraldic shields, and real and imaginary animals hand-coloured in bright shades. There are eight different types of copperplate engraved borders printed on the scroll. They were originally designed by Andrea Marelli, a book illustrator and printmaker who was active in Rome around 1567–72. Marelli's engraved borders were initially used in Latin printed books and might have been adapted to the Esther tale by a creative bookseller. This is one of only three extant scrolls with printed Marelli borders and one of four surviving 16th-century Esther Scrolls.

139 Queen Vashti
Scroll of Esther
Germany
second half of the 18th-century
c. 2000 x 180 mm (length and height of entire scroll)
MS Add. 11832

The spaces above and between the circular columns of text in this scroll are filled with floral and animal designs and naïve drawings of characters from Esther (see also *figs.* 137–8) This opening page featuring a woman dressed in regal attire and a soldier brandishing a sword, depicts the execution of Queen Vashti, as related in the midrashic literature. It is highly likely that Abraham ben Moses, the scribe who copied the biblical text, was also responsible for creating the decorations.

This Esther scroll abounds in original text illustrations confirmed by the addition of Hebrew inscriptions taken from Esther, which the artist was seemingly well-acquainted with. The jesters playing musical instruments on the left and the three upper vignettes on the right represent the merrymaking and distribution of gifts during the *Purim* feast (Esther 8:16 and 9:19). The two ships depicted in the lower margin represent the first known text illustrations in a Hebrew manuscript of the verse, '... upon the isles of the sea...' (Esther 10:1).

140 *Purim* jesters and musicians
Scroll of Esther
probably Holland
c. 1630 or 1640
3800 x 470 mm
(length and height of entire scroll)
MS Or. 1047 (last section of scroll)

141 A decorated *Shiviti* plaque
India?
19th century
110 x 160 mm
MS Or. 14057 (50)

A decorative tablet inscribed with the words, 'I have set [*shiviti*] the Lord always before me...' (Psalm 16:8), is called a *Shiviti*. A *Shiviti* on which the verses of Psalm 67 form a seven-branched candlestick is also known as a *Menorah*, after the Temple Candelabrum. Other typical elements of such votive tablets include kabbalistic inscriptions and variants of the Divine name, such as the 42-letter version here, lending the tablets protective powers. *Shivitis* or *Menorot* are usually hung in synagogues to help worshippers focus on prayer and feel God's presence. They can also be used to protect the home, and as personal amulets. This *Shiviti* names David Suleiman David Sasson as the owner.

In this ornamental *Menorah plaque*, the *Tetragrammaton* or four-letter Divine name, invested with magical powers, is penned in an oval cartouche supported by a pair of rampant yellow lions. The central text, shaped like a candelabrum, is surrounded by the names of angels, as well as biblical, mishnaic and mystical verses believed to protect the owner from harm. (The owner in this case was David Suleiman David Sasson Tsalah, as specified on the reverse side.) *Menorot* or *Shivitis* were often included in prayer books, either loose-leaf or printed within the text. Their appearance in the 17th century was probabaly due to a doctrine that attached deep mystical inpportance to prayer.

142 A *Menorah* plaque
Bombay, India
1891 (date and place on verso)
105 x 155 mm
MS Or. 14057 (114)

Glossay

Ashkenazim Jews originally from Germany, France and England and then more widely from Russia and Eastern Europe.

Covenant The agreement between God and the Jewish people whereby He promised to take care of them if they followed His commandments.

Diaspora The Jewish community worldwide, except for those living in Israel.

Gentiles Jewish term for non-Jews; also known as 'goyim'.

Hagadah, Hagadot Literally 'narration' or 'telling', a collection of holy texts read on Passover eve to commemorate the Jewish Exodus from Egypt.

Hanukah (Festival of Lights) A winter celebration that marks the restoration of the temple by the Maccabees in 164 BC.

Havdalah (meaning 'separation'). A ritual taking place at the close of the Jewish Sabbath.

Hazan Cantor; the person who leads the prayers in a synagogue and intones the liturgy.

Kabbalah An esoteric form of Jewish mysticism. According to Jewish tradition Kabbalah dates from Adam, although modern liberal rabbis date its origins in the 13th century.

Ketubah Marriage document intended to protect the wife's legal and financial rights in case of divorce or widowhood.

Mahzor A Jewish book of festival prayers.

Masorah, masoretic 'Tradition', the traditional way of transmitting a text; hence, the masoretic text, the Hebrew text of the Bible standardized by the scribal editors of the 7th–10th centuries.

Megilat Esther (Scroll of Esther) The name given to the biblical Book of Esther, which is read yearly during the Purim festival.

Menorah Seven-branched candelabrum. One of the oldest symbols in Judaism.

Micrography The practice of using minute script to create abstract shapes or figurative designs.

Mishneh Torah (Repetition of the Law or the Second Law) A legal code compiled by Moses Maimonides (1234–1205).

Parashah A portion of the Torah, one of 54 to cover an annual cycle of Sabbath reading in the synagogue.

Passover A spring festival that marks the Jewish people's escape from captivity in Egypt.

Pentateuch 'Five pieces'; the first five books of the Bible; the Torah.

Purim A festival marking the defeat of an attempt to wipe out the Jews in historical Persia.

Rosh Hashanah Jewish New Year festival.

Sabbath The Jewish day of rest, from sunset on Friday to sunset on Saturday.

Sefer Book; the Sefer Torah is the ceremonial prompt-copy of the Torah in the synagogue.

Sephardim Jews originating from Spain and Portugal.

Shavuot (Festival of Weeks) A harvest festival commemorating the day when Moses received the Torah.

Sidur A Jewish book of daily prayers.

Sofer Scribe; scribal editor.

Sukot (Tabernacles) Festival commemorating the years the Jews spent in the desert on their way to the Promised Land.

Tanakh Acronym of the Hebrew words for the three divisions of the Bible: Torah (Law), Nevi'im (Prophets) and Ketuvim (Writings); a Jewish designation for the Bible.

Targum A translation; specifically an Aramaic translation-paraphrase of a book of the Hebrew Scripture.

Tetragrammaton The name of God reduced to four letters YHWH. It must not be pronounced and is invested with magic powers.

Torah The central document of Judaism, written in Hebrew, and revered by Jews. Also known as the Five Books of Moses or the Pentateuch (i.e. Genesis through to Deuteronomy).

Yom Kipur (Day of Atonement) The most solemn day in the Jewish year when Jews fast and repent for their transgressions.

Further Reading

Beit-Arié, Malachi. *Hebrew Manuscripts of East and West: Towards a Comparative Codicology. The Panizzi Lectures* 1992 (London: the British Library, 1992)

Beit-Arié, Malachi. *Unveiled Faces of Medieval Hebrew Books: The Evolution of Manuscript Production – Progression or Regression?* (Jerusalem: the Hebrew University Magnes Press, 2003)

Cohen, Evelyn M. 'Hebrew manuscript illumination in Italy', in: *Gardens and Ghettos: the Art of Jewish Life in Italy*, edited by Vivian B. Mann, pp. 92–109 (Berkley: University of California Press, 1989)

Frojmovic, Eva. 'Messianic politics in re-Christianized Spain: images of the sanctuary in Hebrew Bible manuscripts', in: *Imagining the Self, Imagining the Other: Visual Representation and Jewish-Christian Dynamics in the Middle Ages and Early Modern Period*, edited by Eva Frojmovic, pp.91–128 (Leiden, Boston: Brill, 2002)

Goldstein, David. *The Ashkenazi Haggadah: A Hebrew Manuscript of the Mid-15th Century from the Collections of the British Library, Written and Illuminated by Joel ben Simeon called Feibusch Ashkenazi…* (London: Thames and Hudson, 1985)

Gutmann, J. *Hebrew Manuscript Painting* (New York: G. Braziller, 1978)

Kogman-Appel, Katrin. *Jewish Book Art Between Islam and Christianity: the Decoration of Hebrew Bibles in Medieval Spain* (Leiden, Boston: Brill, 2004)

Mann, Vivian B. *Art and Ceremony in Jewish life: Essays in the History of Jewish Art* (London: the Pindar Press, 2005)

Namény, E. M. 'La miniature juive au XVIIe et au XVIII siècle', in: *Revue des Études Juives, Nouvelle Serie*, vol. 16, 1957, pp.27–71

Narkiss, Bezalel. *The Golden Haggadah* (London: the British Library, 1997)

Narkiss, Bezalel. *Hebrew Illuminated Manuscripts* (Jerusalem, New York, London, 1969)

Pasternak, Nurit. 'A meeting-point of Hebrew and Latin manuscript production: a fifteenth-century Florentine Hebrew scribe, Isaac ben Ovadia of Forli', in: *Scrittura e Civilta, Roma*, vol. 25 (2001), pp. 185–200

Schrijver, Emile G. L. '"Be-otiyyot Amsterdam": eighteenth-century Hebrew manuscript production in Central Europe: the case of Jacob ben Judah Leib Shamas', in: *Quaerendo: A Quarterly Journal from the Low Countries Devoted to Manuscripts and Printed Books* (Amsterdam, vol. 20, no. 1 (1990), pp. 24–62

Sed-Rajna, Gabrielle. *Lisbon Bible 1482: British Library Or. 2626.* (Tel-Aviv: Nahar-Miskal, 1988)

Sirat, Colette. *Hebrew Manuscripts of the Middle Ages* (Cambridge: Cambridge University Press, 2002)

Tahan, Ilana. 'Manuscript treasures', in: *Treasures of Jewish Heritage: the Jewish Museum, London*, edited by Rickie Burman *et al*, pp. 132–45 (London: Scala, 2006)

Zirlin, Yael. 'The decoration of the miscellany, its iconography and style', in: *The North French Hebrew Miscellany: British Library Add. MS 11639*, edited by Jeremy Schonfield, pp. 74–161 (London: Facsimile Editions, 2003)

Zirlin, Yael. 'Joel meets Johannes: a fifteenth-century Jewish-Christian collaboration in manuscript illumination', in: *Viator, Medieval and Renaissance Studies*, Turnhout, Belgium, vol. 25 (1995), pp. 265–82

Index of Manuscripts

General Index